**HPBooks**

# POLISH
## COOKING

**ANOTHER BEST-SELLING VOLUME FROM HPBooks**

Food Stylist: Carol Flood Peterson; Photography: Cy DeCosse Inc.
Technical Reader: Ewa Cacase

Special thanks to the Polish Imports Galleria, Minneapolis, Minnesota, for the loan of many items for photography.

Notice: The information contained in this book is true and complete to the best of our knowledge. All recommendations are made without any guarantees on the part of the author or Price Stern Sloan. The author and publisher disclaim all liability in connection with the use of this information.

**Published by HPBooks**
A division of Price Stern Sloan, Inc.
360 N. La Cienega Boulevard
Los Angeles, CA 90048
ISBN 0-89586-272-7
Library of Congress Catalog Card Number 85-61027
©1985 HPBooks, Inc.
Printed by Dong-A Printing Co., Ltd., Seoul, Korea
Represented by Codra Enterprises, Torrance, California

7 6 5 4 3

*Cover Photo: Stuffed Cabbage, page 100.*

# INTRODUCTION

Welcome to the wonderful world of Polish cuisine! If you've been here before, you know what a delicious experience it is. If you've never ventured within its boundaries, you're in for an enriching surprise.

As a result of catered "ethnic" wedding receptions and small, late-night neighborhood taverns where frozen, mass-produced pierogies are heated instantly in microwaves, a certain impression of Polish food has developed. Many people of Polish and non-Polish ancestry alike believe that a Polish diet consists entirely of pickles, pierogies, golombkies, duck soup and kielbasa. That's like saying the Irish thrive only on potatoes and soda bread, or the Germans on sauerkraut and hasenpfeffer.

You're going to discover that Polish cookery is not so characteristic as the cuisine of other nations, such as Chinese, French or Italian. While steeped in tradition, Polish cooking also has been strongly influenced by outside forces. People are going to eat whatever they like and whatever is available. They don't particularly care if it's indigenous to Poland. If they prefer a kind of soup more commonly prepared in Russia, they're going to eat that without a passing thought as to where the recipe originated. They simply like good food prepared tastefully. That's what the recipes in this book are all about.

They're what the Poles of today are eating, or at least trying to eat when ingredients are available. Together, the dishes are representative of the fare found in 95 percent of the country's homes and restaurants.

But lest you be deceived, this book is not a catch-all encyclopedia of every dish prepared in Poland. During the volume's assembly, equal time was spent deciding which recipes to exclude.

The criteria for selecting each dish was that the recipe had to be both appetizing and applicable to today's cook. Detailed instructions for preparing "veal head in tomato sauce," or "peacock stew," may be looked for elsewhere, because it's doubtful that such recipes would encourage you to read on. In short, obsolete, unusual or impractical recipes will not be found here.

It's ironic that you'll be able to prepare many Polish recipes more efficiently than cooks in Poland, due to modern kitchen conveniences we take for granted. Many appliances, such as microwave ovens, food processors, slow-cookers, electric mixers and toasters, are all but unheard of by many cooks in Poland.

I grew up on the outskirts of a small village in northeastern Poland, a few miles from the Russian border. Our small farm, with its barn and stockade fence, was like thousands of others scattered across the Polish countryside. We drew all of our water by hand from a deep outside well, then carried it to the house in buckets. We cooked on cast-iron grates and burners over a firebrick stove fueled with pine wood we cut and split ourselves. Baking and cooking in the oven of a wood-fired stove are much more difficult than in easily regulated gas or electric ovens because constant temperatures are difficult to maintain with wood heat. Temperatures are high at first, then gradually drop. Some Polish cookbooks even take the gradual temperature drop into account when giving cooking times.

These recipes are simple, straightforward, tasty and nourishing. And there are a lot more than pierogies and golombkies. Indeed, you're going to find recipes for what the modern and old-time Poles are eating today. This is a true potpourri of dishes that have evolved over the last ten centuries, fashioned by many influences.

---

On preceding page, Easter medley, clockwise from top center: Grandmother's Sweet Bread, page 136; Vegetable Salad, page 52; Beet & Horseradish Relish, page 46; Boneless Pork Loin, page 102; Normandy Turkey, page 94; and Crispy-Crust Cheesecake, page 145.

# Available Ingredients

Grocery stores in Poland are not what they are in Chicago, Toronto, London or Rome. You won't find counters brimming with fresh vegetables, or 23 kinds of frozen fish. Supplies are limited, seasonal and erratic.

A butcher might offer fat back, pork ribs and a few hanks of sausage. Or, he might have nothing. It all depends. Even the famed canned hams are a myth to most Poles—they're produced almost entirely for export. This is not to say there's no meat. Thousands of homes and mini-farms are surrounded by neat picket fences that keep chickens, hogs, sheep, goats, geese and an occasional milking cow from straying. Although meat is a little easier to come by in rural areas, it's still a prized commodity, something to be savored during hard times or on special occasions. And when meat is served, it's often extended as a filling, made into patties or cooked with vegetables in a goulash. Leftover bits and pieces find their way into sausage and cold cuts, such as head cheese and scrapple. Bones are saved for soups. Nothing is wasted.

For vegetables, almost every home, even in larger towns, has a backyard garden of cabbage, potatoes, beets, carrots, onions and cucumbers. Herbs are grown in window boxes, then dried for year-round use.

During spring and especially fall, mushrooms of all kinds sprout like manna throughout the forests. There, men, women and children forage with a passion that can only be believed when witnessed. Mushrooms are pickled, boiled, fried, baked, stuffed and dried, and make their way into dozens of Polish recipes.

Wild blueberries are harvested, as are strawberries, raspberries, cranberries, and miscellaneous fruit and nuts.

The Baltic Sea is a prime source for herring and ocean fish. Freshwater species, such as northern pike, yellow perch, trout and carp, are caught in the country's numerous lakes, rivers and streams.

# Polish History

Poland's northern and southern boundaries are well-defined geographically, and relatively easy to defend. The Baltic Sea is on the north, with the Carpathian and Sudetes Mountains to the south. Trouble has come persistently from the eastern and western borders which have traditionally been minor topographic features, such as small rivers that flow northward to the Baltic, across a wide plain that straddles most of Europe. Over the last thousand years of Polish history, scores of armies—Mongols, Teutonic Knights, Turks, Swedes, Germans, Austrians, Prussians and Russians—thundered across this flat corridor. Time and again, Poland was conquered, occupied, partitioned and reconquered.

But its troubled years were interspersed with times during which the Polish nobility built alliances with the royal courts of other European nations. Indeed, for a while, Poland was looked upon as *the* major power and seat of culture. And intermarriages of Polish aristocracy with French and Italian royalty brought foreign customs and cuisines into play.

Those times, however, were brief. During the 18th century, Austria, Prussia and Russia conquered Poland and divided it among themselves. Although there was no official Polish state during the entire 19th century, the Poles never ceased struggling for their independence. They clung to their customs and ways, battered and challenged as they were by the conquerors.

After World War I, Poland's independence was at last regained, only to be snuffed out several decades later by the brutal Nazi regime. Hitler wanted to Germanize Poland. He planned to annihilate the Polish people and culture completely to make way for those of Germany.

Following World War II, Russia and Poland signed an agreement that actually shifted Poland's boundaries westward. In the east, Poland lost to Russia more than 69,000 square miles and 10 million people. To the west, from

Germany, Poland gained more than 38,000 square miles and 8 million people. Even after the mass migration following the boundary shift, many "half" Germans—still living where their German ancestors had dwelt for generations—discovered that they were living within the newly created Polish state instead of Germany.

Russian influence continued to rise thereafter. It peaked in the early 1950s, when Poland's policies became identical to those of its huge eastern neighbor.

Due largely to its volatile history—a history of wars, partitions and occupations—and somewhat due to the benign foreign influences of milder times, Polish cuisine contains subtle characteristics from the cookery of countries like France, Germany, Italy, Hungary, Russia and many others.

## Religion and Holidays

Most of the Polish people are Roman Catholic. And Polish Catholicism is conservative in the strictest sense. Fridays are still meatless for much of the population, even when meat is available. That, coupled with spartan Lenten fasts, necessitated the development of meatless dishes.

The Catholic faith also gives cause for many celebrations, such as Christmas and Easter feasts, and baptism and wedding gatherings, for which traditional meals have evolved.

Three holidays—Easter, Christmas and New Year's—are especially noteworthy.

**Easter**—In Poland, Easter is the happiest day of the year, when the Catholic Church celebrates the resurrection of Christ, and Poles cap their spartan 40-day Lenten fast with a joyous breakfast feast. Even the countryside reflects the bright and cheerful mood, with larks and other songbirds punctuating the cool mornings with their singing, and flowers of all kinds in bloom amidst lush vegetation.

Throughout Poland, the week before Easter finds housewives busy with spring cleaning and preparing the many dishes that will grace Easter morning tables.

Although traditions vary from North to South Poland, here's how my mother and father and many of their friends celebrated Easter.

After a Good Friday dinner of herring and boiled potatoes with parsley, my mother and the children would decorate hard-cooked eggs. Some of the eggs would be dyed in water in which yellow-onion skins, red-onion skins or beet peelings had been boiled. Others would be covered with intricate designs using beeswax and bright-colored paints.

Saturday was a day to complete preparations for Sunday's breakfast. Our best white linen was placed on the table and decorated with boughs of pine cut in the forest. A half-dozen crystal decanters were arranged on one end of the table, full of sparkling liquors in home-tinted ambers, brilliant reds and deep greens. These, plus as least one bottle of clear vodka and another of pale-yellow egg liquor would provide many toasts to our guests throughout the festivities. Tall vases of pussy willows were placed near the table, while others stood empty, awaiting the tulips and hyacinths that would be picked early Easter morning.

My mother would then fill an Easter basket with hard-cooked eggs, salt and pepper, cold cuts, sausage, wheat bread, slices of babka and mazurka, and a small pascal lamb (the symbol of Jesus) made of butter. She would take the complete basket to church to be blessed. The rest of the prepared foods remained in the refrigerator or root cellar. They included platters of sliced roast beef, roast turkey, roast goose or chicken, roast veal, roast suckling pig, baked ham, fish, sauces, salads, cheesecake with raisins, white-frosted babkas, and a variety of mazurkas.

Sunday, after early-morning Easter mass, my mother would walk the children to the church altar to smell the beautiful flowers and listen to the chirping of canaries hidden in small cages within the altar's Easter foliage. Then home to the breakfast buffet—an open house for neighbors and relatives that lasted most of the day.

At the door, mother would greet our guests, offering wedges of hard-cooked egg and wishes of good health and happiness. Then everyone would share all of the blessed foods from the basket before the main buffet began. At our house, most of the dishes were served chilled, except a clear borscht and a pot of sauerkraut with white sausage.

Easter Monday is a holiday mostly for children. It's a day when godparents bring presents of baskets of candy and fruit, toys or clothes to their godchildren. Youngsters all over Poland eagerly await this day.

The old tradition of *Smingus Dyngus* is also played out this day. This is when a surprising splash of water may await you at any turn, even in your own bed. Beware of overhead balconies or stairwells. Look out for boys in trees or on rooftops. Whatever the circumstance, the dousing with water is always followed by the cheerfully spoken phrase "Smingus Dyngus" or other words meaning "Monday morning pouring water." It provides plenty of fun for youngsters, but worries meticulous housekeepers, stern adults and even teenage girls.

How would you like to be dressed in your only new Easter outfit, leaving home early in the morning for a full day of visiting friends, only to have your brothers throw you into a washtub of cold water?

Now that I look back on it, sometimes Smingus Dyngus wasn't that much fun.

Foodwise, Easter Monday is a lazy kind of day. Pots of bigos simmer on stoves throughout the country, and leftovers are the rule.

**Christmas**—There's something about Christmas Eve in Poland that never fails to brighten the faces of even the grumpiest of all Poles. Its joyous, emotional dinner celebration unites separated families and renews friendships that are often strained by the trying conditions of every-day life. The same neighbors who squabble the rest of the year across picket fences, chasing each other's livestock, leaving each other's gate open, will break bread together at the Christmas table among hearty hugs and tears of joy.

Centuries ago, feudal-estate masters suspended the feudal order on Christmas Eve by inviting their servants to sit with them at the same table. Today, Christmas has continued to be a time when love, friendship and, most of all, forgive-ness reign.

My mother used to say that no one holding a grudge can have a peaceful, happy Christmas. Indeed, in Poland, Christmas is a time when you make up with your enemies, and when you com-fort the sick, the poor and the lonely.

Each year, in a gesture symbolic of the Christ-mas spirit, my mother, like thousands of other housewives, sets an extra place at the Christmas Eve dinner table. She lights a lone candle in the window facing the street. The candle flickers through the darkness in the hopes that Christ, in the form of a stranger, will join the family for dinner. It may also serve as a beacon to help guide the spirit of any family member who could not travel the distance in person.

As a reminder of Christ's humble birthplace, a handful of fresh straw is placed beneath the tradi-tional white-linen tablecloth. Before the meal begins, a prayer of thanks is said. Slim wafers or pieces of unleavened bread similar to communion hosts, impressed with biblical figures of Christ, angels, lambs or Blessed Mary, are passed to each participant. Several wafers are then taken to the barn and fed to the family livestock—another reminder of the Bethlehem stable. Other blessed wafers had already been mailed to far-away rela-tives and friends.

Individuals unaware of Polish customs are often surprised to learn that no meat is served during Christmas Eve dinner. Christmas Eve is a time of strict fasting, the closing hours of a four-week period of penance called *Advent*.

Although dinner is meatless, it doesn't mean the meal isn't a bountiful feast. It begins with at least three different soups, including a meatless borscht, closely followed by three traditional fish entrees of which at least two are carp and pike. A seemingly endless array of appetizers, garnishes and accompaniments, the fruits of several days' preparation, are then served between steaming platters of sauerkraut and meatless pierogies. There are pickled beets, pickled mushrooms, pickled herring and fish in tomato sauce. There's Christmas Babka and spicy oven-browned poppy-seed rolls. It's a grand celebration, much in the tradition of earlier elaborate festivities, or *Wigilias,* that featured 12 full courses of food and drink, representing the 12 apostles of Jesus.

After the meal, without even stopping to clear the leftovers from the dinner table, my family always moved into the living room. There the children trimmed a freshly cut pine tree with help from their grandparents. While we hung candy, fruit, nuts and homemade ornaments on the tree, my mother would fasten strings of dangling, recently baked, sweet-smelling *paczki* to the ceiling.

Then every year, like magic, Santa Claus—who suspiciously resembled an absent, portly uncle—would arrive in a red coat and black boots, carrying a large sack slung over one shoulder. The sack was full of gifts for the children. But it wasn't that easy! We had to work for them. Our Santa would make us sing a song, recite a poem, say a prayer or perform a dance before we could make off with our prizes. All the while, the food remained on the dinner table, with continuous snacking throughout the evening until we went to bed or left for *Pasterka,* Midnight Mass.

To those who didn't attend Midnight Mass, Christmas Day brings church, and a late morning or early afternoon buffet for relatives and friends.

Not much cooking is done on Christmas Day. Instead, it's a peaceful time, a time to relax and nibble on cold turkey and smoked pork loin, ham, veal, meat loaf with hard-cooked eggs, bigos, vegetable salad and clear borscht with dried-mushroom uszka. It's an all-day open house, with neighbors dropping in on one another and snacking on tortes and cheesecakes.

During the afternoon, young people form groups and go caroling through the streets, dressed as kings, shepherds or other biblical characters. If they sing in front of your house and you don't give them food or vodka, they might pull your sleigh five houses down, or remove your fence gate—all in good humor.

New Year's—New Year's Eve in Poland is similar to New Year's Eve throughout much of the world. Dances held in restaurants, schools and auditoriums feature plenty of good companionship, music, drink and food. Appetizers, both hot and cold, are prepared and brought by partygoers who share their creations with everyone at their table. It's the biggest, wildest party in Poland.

The following day, though, has a tradition all its own: the *kulig.* Throughout the countryside, shaggy brown-maned plowhorses are hitched to sleighs or wagons piled high with hay. Then off go the sturdy steeds, snorting, prancing into the dusk along snow-covered forest trails, with sleigh bells jingling in the crisp air. They pull their passengers to a place in the forest where a bonfire is started and sausage is roasted next to a simmering pot of bigos. Beer and vodka flow freely, and stories are told long into the night.

## The Social Nature of the Poles

Perhaps because the average Pole is not so mobile as his western cousin, most Polish entertaining is done at home, with relatives or close friends. As you have already read, at these intimate parties, meals play a central role. The Pole is a notorious nibbler and muncher. While playing cards, watching television or simply engaging in conversation, he'll often forego the main meal to pick at a variety of side dishes developed especially for entertaining. These are served along with relishes, pickled herring, mushrooms, cucumbers or peppers, thin-sliced smoked pork loin, cheese, rolls, rye bread and the inevitable pastries. It's one small platter after another throughout the evening, each chased with tea, soda, wine, beer or vodka.

Many family cooks in Poland don't follow written recipes. Instead, they cook by "feel" and taste—adding so much of this and so much of that. Unfortunately, this method produces almost as many unaccomplished cooks as it does good ones. So, to begin with at least, I recommend that you stick to the traditional recipes. Later, feel free to experiment with them. If you like more salt, pepper, paprika or sour cream, fine. But remember to keep accurate records so you can duplicate any variations you'd like to prepare again.

When you are with family and friends and sit down to a meal based on recipes from this book, you can also share some of the information about Polish history and customs. Why not? When you pass the pierogies, pass along some Polish tradition as well.

Sincerely,

Marianna Olszewska Heberle

 Marianna Olszewska Heberle, a native of Suwalki, Poland, currently resides with her husband and two daughters in Erie, Pennsylvania. She was brought up on a small farm in a village in northeastern Poland, not far from the Russian border. There she frequently assumed household cooking responsibilities while her parents and brothers worked in the fields. Often, Marianna cooked at her grandmother's side, learning many old-time recipes and techniques at an early age.

After moving to the United States, Marianna worked as a supermarket delicatessen operator, cooked for and catered private dinner parties, wrote and published *A Pierogi Handbook,* and gave lectures and cooking demonstrations at the Cracow Festival at Alliance College, the college of the Polish National Alliance in Cambridge Springs, Pennsylvania.

Marianna frequently shares both her culinary skills and the results of those skills with close friends and acquaintances, and is an active participant in many Polish-sponsored functions in her community. Through this book, she hopes to share some of Poland and its native cuisine with you.

# APPETIZERS

When I was a child, I remember traveling by train once a year to visit my aunt in Steczyn for our annual family gathering. Each year, my brothers and I made a contest of guessing what main dish my aunt would prepare for dinner.

It was a contest rarely decided until the following morning. And then it was only by hearsay because most of us found it impossible to stay hungry and awake through the marathon-like appetizer courses, and the many hours of socializing that always preceded dinner.

Every year, upon our arrival in late afternoon, out would come platter after platter of *zakaski*. These Polish appetizers were served cheerfully by my aunt and her daughters. There were many types of cold fish: herring, northern pike, trout and carp—smoked, pickled, salted and marinated in sour-cream sauces. There were attractively arranged plates of sliced, cold-smoked pork loin, kielbasa, chicken, tongue and other specialty meats. And no party was without the lettuce-lined trays of pig's feet and cooked fish served chilled in a flavorful gelatin aspic.

Many other bite-sized morsels were also provided. They included homemade crackers, cold and hot stuffed hard-cooked eggs and mushrooms, pickled onions and mushrooms, chunks of soft and hard cheeses, and slices of crisp fresh vegetables.

The ever-present *ogorek*, or dill pickle, was there, too. It was sliced lengthwise, served in a dish next to pickled red sweet peppers or pimentos.

Round and round the table these appetizers went, a free-for-all limited only by what my aunt could find at market and by her fertile imagination. And when one plate was cleaned, another—with an entirely different snack—was brought in its place.

All the while conversation flowed freely, often aided by a generous supply of Polish spiritus or vodka. Thus, the hours passed and, little by little, we children succumbed to the constant nibbling until we could eat no more and our eyelids grew heavy.

Even among the older children who attempted to save room and energy for dinner, all hopes

## Steak Tartare

Befsztyk Tatarski

*Be sure beef is very lean as fat is not appetizing in tartare.*

**1 lb. lean beef top round or sirloin**
**6 egg yolks**
**1 teaspoon onion powder**
**1 teaspoon salt**

**1/4 teaspoon freshly ground black pepper**
**1 teaspoon vegetable oil**
**1/4 cup chopped fresh chives**

Using a grinder or food processor fitted with a metal blade, process beef until finely minced. Process a second time. Do not puree. In a medium bowl, combine beef, egg yolks, onion powder, salt, pepper and oil. Cover with foil; refrigerate at least 1 hour. Garnish with chives. Serve as a side dish or a spread with crackers, bread or toast. Makes 6 side-dish servings or 12 appetizers.

were dashed with the arrival of the *kanapki,* or canapés. These traditional Polish creations followed the initial rounds of appetizers as sure as the Russian guards relieve each other at the Lenin Building in Warsaw Square.

As mentioned earlier, Poles are notorious munchers, capable of holding a social event around a dish of cottage cheese sprinkled with chopped chives. To that end, canapés are a muncher's dream—a little of this, a little of that; some sour, some sweet; some vegetable, some meat.

Like the zakaski, kanapki are prepared almost entirely without official rules. It can be said only that they're made with small squares or rounds of white, rye or wheat bread. A variety of pâtés, sauces, dressings and flavored butters are spread over the bite-sized breads. Then they're topped with ingredients such as sardines, chopped herring, anchovies, sprats, hard-cooked-egg slices, cheeses, cold meats, pickled mushrooms, tomatoes, green onions, horseradish, pickled beets and sliced vegetables. The list runs on and on. In short, kanapki can be thought of as dainty sandwiches without the tops, often impaled by wooden picks for easy handling and serving.

They're usually served cold, but sometimes, when the mood strikes the host's fancy, they can be prepared and served hot.

# Canapés with Eggs

Kanapki z Jajkami

*Keep hard-cooked eggs on hand for this quick-to-fix appetizer.*

**3 tablespoons butter or margarine,
   room temperature**
**20 thin slices French bread**
**1/4 cup chopped fresh chives**

**Salt**
**4 hard-cooked eggs**
**Mayonnaise, page 53, or other mayonnaise**
**Ground sweet paprika**

Spread butter or margarine on 1 side of each bread slice. Sprinkle with chives. Season with salt to taste. Cut 1/4 inch off both ends of each egg. Carefully slice each egg crosswise into 5 equal slices. Place 1 egg slice on each buttered bread slice. Spoon mayonnaise into a pastry bag fitted with a medium fluted nozzle. Pipe mayonnaise onto egg slices. Garnish with paprika. Arrange on a platter. Makes 20 appetizers.

## Variation

Place bite-sized pieces of sliced, peeled cucumber, smoked ham or sausage on mayonnaise flowers.

# Stuffed Swirls

Ptysie

*A delicious dessert when filled with a sweet cream or pudding.*

**1 cup water**
**1/2 cup butter or margarine**
**1/2 teaspoon salt**
**1 cup all-purpose flour**
**5 medium eggs**

**2 tablespoons butter or margarine**
**2 medium onions, minced**
**1 lb. fresh mushrooms, minced**
**1 tablespoon dairy sour cream**

Preheat oven to 400F (205C). Grease and lightly flour a large baking sheet. Combine water, 1/2 cup butter or margarine and salt in a medium saucepan. Bring to a boil over medium heat. Add flour all at once. Stir vigorously with a wooden spoon until smooth and dough forms a ball and leaves side of pan. Remove from heat. Add eggs, 1 at a time, stirring until smooth after each addition. Spoon dough into a large pastry bag fitted with a large fluted nozzle. Pipe dollops of dough, about 1 tablespoon each, onto prepared baking sheet, leaving room for spreading. Bake 20 to 25 minutes or until golden brown. Let cool. Melt 2 tablespoons butter or margarine in a large skillet. Add onions and mushrooms; sauté over medium-low heat until tender. Stir sour cream into onion mixture; let cool. Cut baked pastry swirls in 1/2 horizontally. Using a spoon or small paring knife, remove any soft dough inside puffs, leaving a hollow, 2-part shell or crust about 1/4 to 3/8 inch thick. Spoon about 1 tablespoon sour-cream mixture in bottom portion of each swirl. Replace top portion of swirls. Preheat oven to 350F (175C). Bake on a large baking sheet 10 minutes or until heated through. Makes about 25.

# Torte Canapés

Tort Kanapkowy

*Firm, heavy loaves of bakery bread work best for this recipe.*

Meat Spread, see below
Green Spread, see below
Herring Spread, see below

Tomato Spread, see below
Onion Spread, see below
1 loaf Polish or German rye bread, unsliced

*Meat Spread:*
1/2 cup ground cooked chicken, pork,
    veal or beef

2 tablespoons butter or margarine

*Green Spread:*
2 tablespoons chopped fresh parsley or
    chives
1-1/2 tablespoons butter or margarine

1 tablespoon lemon juice
Pinch of salt

*Herring Spread:*
2 hard-cooked eggs, chopped
1 herring-in-oil fillet, drained, chopped

*Tomato Spread:*
1 (3-oz.) pkg. cream cheese,
    room temperature
2 teaspoons tomato paste

1 garlic clove, crushed
Pinch of salt

*Onion Spread:*
1/2 medium onion, chopped
1 dill pickle, chopped
1 tablespoon dairy sour cream

1 tablespoon shredded sharp Cheddar cheese
Several drops red food coloring or
    1/4 teaspoon beet juice

Prepare spreads. Slice off ends and trim top, bottom and side crusts of bread as needed. Cut trimmed bread into 6 (1/2-inch-thick) horizontal slices. Remove top bread slice from stack; set aside. Place a thin layer of each spread on the 5 remaining bread slices. Stack bread layers in their original positions. Top with remaining slice, then gently press layers together. Cut stacked loaf into serving-size squares or triangles. Makes 16 to 20 appetizers.

**Spreads:**
Using a blender or food processor fitted with a metal blade, process ingredients for each spread into a smooth paste.

# How to Make Stuffed Egg Shells

1/Holding a folded towel in one hand, place egg lengthwise on towel. With a heavy, sharp knife, split egg lengthwise halfway through, with a firm stroke of the knife.

2/Place egg and towel on a clean surface. Firmly cut through the egg so shell does not break apart. Repeat with remaining eggs.

3/Prepare egg filling. Carefully spoon equal amounts of egg mixture into each egg-shell half.

4/Dip flat surface of each stuffed egg shell in bread crumbs. Place stuffed egg shells, flat-side down, in skillet with melted butter or margarine.

# Stuffed Egg Shells

Jaja Faszerowane

*For Easter, use decorated eggs to prepare these unique appetizers.*

3 hard-cooked eggs, unpeeled
2 tablespoons dairy sour cream
2 tablespoons dry bread crumbs
1 tablespoon chopped green onion

Salt
Freshly ground black pepper
2 tablespoons butter or margarine

Fold a cloth towel in several layers. Holding the towel in 1 hand, place 1 unpeeled egg on towel. Hold egg lengthwise. With a heavy, sharp knife, split egg lengthwise halfway through with a firm stroke of the knife. Firmly cut the rest of the way through so shell does not break apart. Repeat with remaining eggs. Carefully remove egg whites and yolks from shells. Reserve shells intact. In a small bowl, chop egg whites and yolks together. Stir in sour cream, 1 tablespoon bread crumbs and green onion. Season to taste with salt and pepper. Carefully pack equal amounts of egg mixture into each egg shell. Place remaining bread crumbs on a small plate. Dip flat surface of each stuffed egg shell in bread crumbs. Lightly press bread crumbs into egg mixture. Melt butter or margarine in a medium skillet. Place stuffed egg shells, flat-side down, in skillet. Cook over medium heat 2 to 3 minutes or until lightly browned. Serve immediately. Makes 6 appetizers.

# Ham & Egg Wraps

Jaja Zawijane w Szynce

*For a fast appetizer, serve these simple, tasty treats.*

3 hard-cooked eggs
12 (5" x 1") thin slices ham
Small cooked or pickled onions, pickled
　　red-sweet-pepper slices, chives
　　or anchovies

Peel and quarter eggs. Wrap a ham slice around each egg quarter, leaving egg ends showing. Secure ham with a wooden pick. Garnish with onions, pepper slices, chives or anchovies. Makes 12 appetizers.

# Egg Spread

Pasta z Jaj

*A tasty spread, great for stuffing cucumbers or tomatoes.*

4 hard-cooked eggs
1/3 lb. thinly sliced baked ham
2 tablespoons vegetable oil

Ground sweet paprika
Salt

In a grinder or food processor fitted with a metal blade, process eggs and ham until finely ground. Do not puree. In a small bowl, combine eggs, ham, oil and paprika. Season to taste with salt. Makes about 1-1/2 cups.

# Mushroom Rounds

Paszteciki z Pieczarkami

*Serve these delicious hot appetizers for any occasion.*

Dough 1, see below
Dough 2, see below
1 egg white, lightly beaten
1 egg yolk, lightly beaten
2 tablespoons butter or margarine

1/2 lb. fresh mushrooms, minced
3 tablespoons half and half
1/4 teaspoon all-purpose flour
1/8 teaspoon salt
Pinch of freshly ground black pepper

*Dough 1:*
2/3 cup all-purpose flour
1 egg yolk

2 tablespoons dairy sour cream
1/4 cup water

*Dough 2:*
2/3 cup all-purpose flour
1/2 cup plus 1 tablespoon butter or
  margarine, room temperature

Prepare each dough. On a lightly floured board, roll out Dough 1 into a rectangle about 1/4 inch thick. Place 1 ball Dough 2 on center of rolled dough rectangle. Gently press dough ball with your hands or rolling pin until dough ball is 1/4 inch thick and covers a circular portion of Dough 1. Fold up both short sides of Dough 1 over rolled Dough 2 so ends meet in center. Re-roll resulting dough combination into a rectangle 1/4 inch thick. Repeat with remaining 2 balls of dough 2. Roll dough jelly-roll style. Wrap dough in foil; refrigerate overnight. Preheat oven to 400F (205C). Grease a baking sheet. Halve dough crosswise. On a lightly floured board, roll out 1/2 of dough into a rectangle 1/4 to 3/8 inch thick. Using a round 2-inch cutter, cut dough rounds. Arrange 16 rounds on greased baking sheet, allowing room for spreading. Press leftover dough scraps into a ball. Roll to same thickness; cut as many dough rounds as possible. Repeat process with remaining dough until a total of 48 rounds are cut. With a 1-inch round cutter, cut out centers of 32 dough rounds not on baking sheets, forming doughnut shapes. Using a pastry brush, apply beaten egg white to top surface of 1 uncut dough round on baking sheet. Carefully position 1 doughnut cutout directly on top of brushed dough round. Lightly press doughnut cutout down with your fingertips. Brush egg white on top of doughnut cutout. Place a second doughnut cutout on top of the first. Pat lightly with your fingertips. Repeat process until all dough rounds on baking sheet have 2 doughnut cutouts "glued" on. Brush beaten egg yolk on top of doughnut cutouts. Bake 15 minutes or until golden; let cool. Melt butter or margarine in a small skillet. Add mushrooms; sauté until nearly tender. In a small bowl, combine half and half, flour, salt and pepper; stir mixture into sautéed mushrooms. Simmer 5 minutes. Set aside to cool. Fill each dough round with about 1 teaspoon cooled mushroom mixture. Bake 8 to 10 minutes. Serve hot. Makes 16 appetizers.

**Dough 1:**
In a medium bowl, combine flour, egg yolk, sour cream and water. Work into a soft, elastic dough. Knead 15 to 20 minutes. Cover; set aside.

**Dough 2:**
In a medium bowl, combine flour and butter or margarine into a smooth, soft dough. Divide dough into 3 balls. Cover dough balls; set aside.

# Pickled Mushrooms

Marynowane Pieczarki

*For best results, use small button mushrooms for this lip-smacking appetizer.*

Marinade, see below
3 cups water

2 tablespoons salt
2 lbs. fresh mushrooms

*Marinade:*
1-1/4 cups white vinegar
10 black peppercorns

2 bay leaves

Prepare Marinade. In a large saucepan, combine water and salt; bring to a boil. Add mushrooms. Cover tightly and simmer over low heat 10 minutes. Strain mushrooms; discard cooking liquid. Let cool. Arrange equal amounts of mushrooms in 2 (1-pint) canning jars. Pour boiling marinade over mushrooms to cover. Place lids on jars; seal tightly. Let cool to room temperature; refrigerate. Serve chilled. Makes 2 pints.

**Marinade:**
Simmer vinegar, peppercorns and bay leaves in a small covered saucepan 10 minutes over medium-low heat. Bring to a boil over medium heat.

# Stuffed Mushrooms

Pieczarki Nadziewane

*Poles say "Caps off" to this favorite appetizer.*

20 (1-1/2- to 2-inch) fresh mushrooms
   (about 1 lb.)
2 tablespoons butter or margarine
1 small onion, minced
3 tablespoons dry bread crumbs
1 tablespoon dairy sour cream
1 hard-cooked egg, minced

1 egg
1 tablespoon chopped fresh parsley
1/4 teaspoon salt
1/8 teaspoon freshly ground black pepper
20 (1-inch) squares thinly sliced Gouda or
   Swiss cheese

Preheat oven to 400F (205C). Grease a 9- or 10-inch-square baking dish. Separate mushroom stems and caps; set caps aside. Finely chop stem pieces. Melt butter or margarine in a small skillet over medium heat. Add onion; sauté until soft, about 3 minutes. In a small bowl, combine sautéed onion, chopped mushroom stems, bread crumbs, sour cream and hard-cooked egg. In a small bowl, beat egg with a fork. Add to onion mixture. Stir in parsley, salt and pepper until blended. Pack about 1 rounded teaspoon stuffing mixture into each reserved mushroom cap. Arrange, stuffing-side up, in greased dish. Place 1 cheese square on each cap. Bake, uncovered, 20 to 25 minutes. Makes 20 appetizers.

# How to Make Toast with Sprats

1/Remove sprats from oil; drain well. Clean sprats by gently pulling off tails and backbones.

2/Evenly spread 1 teaspoon sprat mixture on buttered bread. Top each with cheese, then sprinkle with parsley.

## Toast with Sprats

Grzanki z Szprotka

*Sprats are small fish, similar to sardines, canned and packed in oil.*

**8 oz. canned smoked sprats**
**1/4 cup milk**
**1 soft dinner roll**
**2 tablespoons dairy sour cream**
**1 tablespoon lemon juice**
**1/4 teaspoon salt**

**1/8 teaspoon freshly ground black pepper**
**6 slices white or rye bread**
**6 thin slices mozzarella cheese**
**2 tablespoons butter or margarine,**
   **room temperature**
**Chopped fresh parsley**

Preheat oven to 450F (230C). Remove sprats from oil; drain well. Clean sprats by gently pulling off tails and backbones. In a small bowl, mash sprats with a fork. Place milk in a shallow bowl. Break roll into pieces; soak roll pieces in milk. Combine soaked roll and sprats with a fork. Stir in sour cream and lemon juice. Season with salt and pepper. Trim off bread crusts. Cut each bread slice into 4 triangles. Diagonally cut each cheese slice into triangles. Spread butter or margarine on both sides of each bread slice. Arrange bread slices on a baking sheet. Evenly spread about 1 teaspoon sprat mixture on each buttered bread slice. Top each with a piece of cheese. Sprinkle parsley over cheese. Bake 4 to 5 minutes or until lightly browned. Serve hot. Makes 24 appetizers.

# Meat Pâté

Pasztet

*A popular pâté to serve on canapés, sandwiches or other appetizers.*

| | |
|---|---|
| 1 lb. veal | Salt |
| 3/4 lb. fatty pork from leg or shoulder | 1 lb. beef liver |
| 1/2 lb. beef chuck | 3/4 cup milk |
| 2 celery stalks | 3 stale dinner rolls |
| 1 parsley root, halved | 3 eggs |
| 3 medium onions | 1 teaspoon salt |
| 4 medium carrots, halved | 1/4 teaspoon freshly ground black pepper |
| 2 bay leaves | 1/4 teaspoon ground nutmeg |
| 1/2 tablespoon dried leaf marjoram | 2 tablespoons fine dry bread crumbs |
| 8 black peppercorns | 8 crisp-cooked bacon slices |
| 7 dried mushrooms, soaked | Lettuce leaves |
| Water | |

Place veal, pork, beef, celery, parsley root, onions, carrots, bay leaves, marjoram, peppercorns and mushrooms in a large pot. Add enough salted water to cover. Bring to a boil over high heat. Reduce heat to low. Simmer, partially covered, 1-1/2 to 2 hours. Add beef liver. Simmer, partially covered, 1 hour. Strain, reserving cooking juices. Discard celery, parsley root, onions, carrots, bay leaves and peppercorns. Place milk in a shallow bowl. Break rolls into pieces; soak roll pieces in milk. Using a grinder, grind cooked veal, pork, beef, mushrooms, liver and soaked rolls into a large bowl. Grind resulting mixture a second time. Add eggs, 1 teaspoon salt, pepper and nutmeg; stir to blend. If mixture is not moist enough, add a little reserved cooking juices. Preheat oven to 350F (175C). Grease 2 (8" x 4") loaf pans. Sprinkle each greased pan with 1 tablespoon bread crumbs. Arrange 4 crisp bacon slices on bottom of each pan. Place equal amounts of meat mixture in each pan. Bake 40 to 50 minutes or until mixture sets and sides of meat mixture pull away from pan sides. Remove from oven; cool. To serve, slice pâté in pans or turn out of pans to slice. Line a serving plate with lettuce leaves. Arrange pâté slices on lined serving plate. Makes 2 loaves.

# Smoked-Fish Spread

Pasta Rybna

*Use any smoked fish to prepare this favorite canapé spread.*

| | |
|---|---|
| 1/2 lb. smoked-fish fillets | Salt |
| 1/4 cup minced leek | Ground white pepper |
| 2 tablespoons Mayonnaise, page 53, or other mayonnaise | Fresh bread, toast or crackers |

In a food processor fitted with a metal blade, puree smoked fish. Or, place fish on a flat working surface; mash with a fork. Place pureed or mashed fish in a medium bowl. Stir in leeks and mayonnaise. Season with salt and white pepper to taste. Cover and refrigerate 30 minutes. Serve chilled on fresh bread, toast or crackers. Makes about 1-1/3 cups.

# Warsaw Herring

Sledz po Warszawsku

*Serve this attractive appetizer in a clear-glass dish.*

2 lbs. small salted dressed herring
1/2 cup cold milk
2 tablespoons prepared mustard
1 medium dill pickle, finely shredded
1 medium apple, peeled, finely shredded
1 medium onion, shredded

1/2 pickled sweet red pepper or pimento,
   minced
1/4 teaspoon freshly ground black pepper
2 medium onions, thinly sliced
1 cup olive oil
Pimento strips for garnish

In a large bowl, place herring in enough cold water to cover. Soak 6 to 8 hours, changing water 3 times. Bone herring; remove skin. Cut each herring lengthwise into 2 fillets. Place fillets in a narrow baking dish. Pour milk over herring. Let stand at room temperature 1 hour, turning herring several times. Remove from milk; pat dry. Discard milk. On a flat working surface, arrange fillets. Spread mustard evenly over tops of fillets. In a medium bowl, combine dill pickle, apple, shredded onion, red pepper or pimento, and black pepper. Spread equal amounts of dill-pickle mixture on fillets. Roll fillets, lengthwise, jelly-roll style. Secure with wooden picks. Place 1/2 sliced onions on bottom of a medium glass or ceramic jar or crock. Add herring rolls. Top with remaining onions. Drizzle oil over onions and herring. Cover; refrigerate 2 to 3 days. To serve, arrange herring rolls on a plate or in a clear-glass dish. Garnish with pimento strips. Let stand 1 hour at room temperature. Makes 12 to 16 servings.

### Variation

If using small herring, layer herring rolls in a serving dish.

# Marinated Herring     Photo on pages 126 & 127.

Marynowane Sledzie

*A popular herring dish in Poland, often prepared for special occasions and meatless holidays.*

1 cup white vinegar
1 cup water
5 black peppercorns
5 allspice berries
2 bay leaves, crushed

2 large onions, thinly sliced
2 lbs. fresh dressed herring
2 or 3 herring milt sacs
3 tablespoons olive oil

In a medium saucepan, combine vinegar, water, peppercorns, allspice and bay leaves. Bring to a boil. Cook, uncovered, over medium heat 5 minutes. Add onions; reduce heat and simmer 3 minutes. Remove from heat; let cool. Drain onions, reserving vinegar mixture. Cut herring into 1-1/2- to 3-inch pieces. In a medium glass or ceramic jar, or crock with a tight-fitting lid, arrange 1 layer of herring. Top with a thin layer of cooked onions. Repeat layering process until all herring and onions are used. In a small bowl, crush milt sacs. Stir into reserved vinegar mixture. Pour vinegar mixture over herring. Drizzle oil over herring. Cover with tight-fitting lid. Gently shake jar or crock to evenly distribute vinegar mixture and oil. Refrigerate 3 to 4 days before serving. Makes 12 to 16 servings.

Warsaw Herring

# Onion Rolls

Cebulak

*Great to serve with soup or salad, or as a hearty appetizer.*

Onion Filling, see below
2 (1/4-oz.) pkgs. active dry yeast
   (2 tablespoons)
1/2 cup warm water (110F, 45C)
2 tablespoons plus 3 cups all-purpose flour

1 teaspoon sugar
3/4 cup warm milk
1/4 teaspoon salt
1/4 teaspoon ground nutmeg
1 egg

*Onion Filling:*
2 tablespoons butter or margarine
4 large onions, minced
   (about 3 to 3-1/2 cups)

1/2 teaspoon salt
1/4 teaspoon freshly ground black pepper

Prepare Onion Filling. In a small bowl, dissolve yeast in 1/4 cup warm water. Stir in 2 tablespoons flour, sugar and milk. Let stand until foamy, 5 to 10 minutes. Place remaining 3 cups flour, salt and nutmeg in a large bowl. In a small bowl, beat 1 egg and remaining 1/4 cup water; stir into yeast mixture. Add mixture to dry ingredients. Stir or knead mixture into a pliable dough. Turn out dough onto a lightly floured surface. Clean and grease bowl. Knead dough 8 to 10 minutes or until smooth and elastic. Place dough in greased bowl, turning to coat all sides. Cover with a damp cloth. Let rise in a warm place, free from drafts, until doubled in bulk, about 2 hours. Grease 2 baking sheets. Divide dough into 4 parts. Roll out 1 part dough on an unfloured work surface until 1/8 to 1/4 inch thick. Using a round 4-inch cutter, cut out dough. Place 1 teaspoon Onion Filling on center of 1 dough round. Spread to within 1/2 inch of edge. Roll jelly-roll style. Place onion roll, seam-side down, on greased baking sheet. With your fingers, sharply bend ends of onion roll together until they touch each other, like a fortune cookie. Pinch to seal. Repeat process with remaining dough and Onion Filling until baking sheet is filled, leaving enough space between rolls for rising. Cover with a cloth. Let rise in a warm place, free from drafts, until doubled in bulk, about 1 hour. Preheat oven to 350F (175C). Bake 20 to 25 minutes or until golden brown. Makes 36 to 40 rolls.

**Onion Filling:**
Melt butter or margarine in a medium skillet. Add onions; sauté over medium heat until tender. Season with salt and pepper. Let cool.

# Ham Triangles

Grzanki z Szynka

*A fast, snappy appetizer to serve hot at parties.*

1/4 cup minced ham
2 tablespoons grated provolone or
   Gouda cheese
2 tablespoons dairy sour cream

4 slices slightly stale bread
2 tablespoons butter or margarine,
   room temperature

Preheat oven to 450F (230C). In a small bowl, combine ham, cheese and sour cream. Cut each bread slice into 4 triangles. Spread butter or margarine on both sides of bread triangles; arrange on a baking sheet. Spread ham mixture evenly on top of each bread triangle. Bake 10 to 12 minutes or until browned. Makes 16 appetizers.

# How to Make Onion Rolls

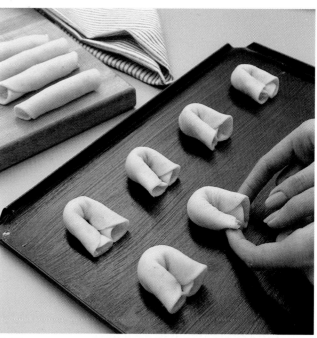

1/Roll out dough on an unfloured surface. Cut out 4-inch rounds of dough. Place 1 teaspoon filling on center of each round. Spread to within 1/2 inch of the edge. Roll jelly-roll style.

2/Place onion roll, seam-side down, on greased baking sheet. With your fingers, sharply bend ends of onion roll together until they touch each other, like a fortune cookie. Pinch to seal.

# Chicken Pâté

Pasztet z Kury

*A grinder will help give the correct consistency for this popular spread.*

**4 cups water**
**Salt**
**1 (2- to 2-1/2-lb.) chicken, cut up**
**1/4 lb. chicken livers**
**1/4 lb. fresh bacon, chopped**

**2 stale dinner rolls**
**2 eggs, beaten**
**1/2 teaspoon ground nutmeg**
**Freshly ground black pepper**

Heat water and 1/2 teaspoon salt in a large deep skillet. Add chicken, livers and bacon. Bring to a boil over medium-high heat. Cover with a tight-fitting lid. Reduce heat to medium-low. Cook 1 hour or until chicken is tender. Remove chicken, livers and bacon from cooking liquid; let cool. Reserve cooking liquid. Preheat oven to 350F (175C). Grease a 9'' x 5'' loaf pan. Remove bones and skin from chicken. Break rolls into pieces. Soak roll pieces in reserved cooking liquid until moistened; squeeze out excess juice. Grind cooked chicken, livers, bacon and soaked rolls into a large bowl. Grind resulting mixture a second time. Blend in beaten eggs and nutmeg. Season with salt and pepper to taste. Place chicken mixture in greased pan; pat smooth. Bake, uncovered, 1 hour or until pâté is firm; let cool. Cover; refrigerate 48 hours. Makes 1 loaf.

# SOUPS

My grandmother used to boast that she could make a pot of soup every day for three consecutive months without ever preparing the same soup twice. Although we never challenged her to try it, we never had reason to doubt her.

Soups are very important in the daily Polish diet. You'll find a variety in this chapter unlike those served regularly in the West. In addition to "conventional" soups, such as Chicken, Vegetable and Tomato, Poles love sour soups made with dill pickles or sauerkraut. Or sweet dessert-like soups created from a host of fresh and dried fruits. Other popular soups include Barley-Vegetable Soup; Borscht, a delectable combination of meat and beet flavors; the ever-present Fish Soup; and a variety of cream soups thickened with sour cream and roux.

Tripe Soup is a Polish specialty, the mere mention of which will practically bring tears of longing to any Pole. Thoughts of the flavorful soups made from dried and fresh mushrooms cause similar reactions.

There's even one dish called Nothing Soup, so named because it's made with neither meat nor vegetables. It has a wonderful taste, similar to that of custard. Children and others with a sweet tooth love it.

The Polish cook frequently garnishes her creations with home-grown herbs and greens. Chopped fresh parsley, chives and dill top the list.

Root-vegetables play an important role in Polish stocks and soups. In addition to beets and carrots, two traditional roots are used that are relatively unknown to Western cooks. One is called *parsley root* or *turnip-rooted parsley*. It's a member of the parsley family that expends most of its energy developing a taproot similar to a white-skinned carrot or parsnip. For centuries, parsley root has been used as a flavoring agent by European cooks, especially German, Hungarian and Polish. Its leaves are larger and softer than the common sprig parsley found in most stores throughout the West. When minced, the leaves make an excellent and attractive garnish.

The other is called *celery root, celeriac, knob* or

# Refreshing Strawberry Soup

Zupa Truskawkowa

*For a Polish fruit drink on a hot summer day, chill this sweet soup.*

1 qt. fresh strawberries
1-3/4 cups water
2 tablespoons sugar

1 tablespoon lemon juice
1 cup half and half
1-1/2 cups cooked egg noodles, if desired

Reserve 4 whole strawberries; slice remaining strawberries. Place sliced strawberries and water in a medium saucepan. Bring to a boil over medium heat. Simmer, uncovered, over low heat 30 minutes. Puree in a blender or food processor fitted with a metal blade. Pour mixture back into medium saucepan. Stir in sugar and lemon juice. Add half and half. Simmer over low heat about 5 minutes; do not boil. Serve hot over noodles, if desired. Or serve chilled. Garnish with reserved whole strawberries. Makes 4 servings.

*turnip-rooted celery.* It's a strange-looking vegetable, much like a bewhiskered turnip. Its globular root mass is the size and shape of a large plum, with many gnarled warts and thread-like roots trailing from its bottom. It gains respectability when trimmed, and has a wonderful celery flavor.

In the West, parsley root and celery root are available in some large produce departments and specialty or ethnic stores. They can be grown in almost any location with soil and weather suitable for carrots or parsnips.

When parsley root isn't available, substitute several bunches of common parsley. If the recipe calls for the root to be ground, mashed or shredded, use parsnips. Although the resulting flavor will not be the same, it probably will be acceptable to all but the most demanding purists.

Celery root is the rarer of the two vegetables. If it isn't available, substitute three or four celery stalks. Parsnips can also be used here, if desired.

When meat is not available, items such as plain and stuffed dumplings, noodles, barley, rice or vegetables can help turn a simple broth or soup into a nourishing main dish.

In recent years, it has not been uncommon for a Polish family to partake of soup four times in one day—breakfast, lunch, dinner and supper. Dinner *and* supper? The typical Pole eats somewhat less per meal than his Western counterpart. However, to make up the difference, Poles eat more often. Instead of three meals per day, the Polish love of food has demanded four. Soup plays an important role in all of them.

# Cherry Soup

Zupa Wisniowa

*Children love this soup.*

4 cups pitted dark sweet cherries
1 pint water (2 cups)
Lemon juice

3 tablespoons sugar
1 pint whipping cream (2 cups)
3 cups cooked egg noodles, if desired

In a large saucepan, combine cherries and water. Bring to a boil over medium heat. Puree cherries and water in a blender or food processor fitted with a metal blade. Return mixture to saucepan. Add lemon juice to taste, sugar and whipping cream. Gently stir until smooth. Serve hot over noodles, if desired. Or serve chilled. Makes 6 servings.

### Variation

Substitute red tart cherries for sweet cherries. Do not add lemon juice. Sweeten with sugar to taste.

# Nothing Soup

Zupa Nic

*One of the few soups you can prepare for dessert.*

3 eggs, separated
3/4 cup sugar
5 cups milk

1 tablespoon Vanilla Sugar, page 136
Pinch of salt
Ground cinnamon

In a medium bowl, beat egg whites until stiff but not dry. Fold in 1/4 cup sugar. In a medium saucepan, combine milk and vanilla sugar. Bring to a boil over medium heat. Add 1 teaspoon egg-white mixture. When milk mixture comes to a boil again and egg white becomes like a dumpling, add another teaspoon egg-white mixture. Wait several seconds. Gently stir, turning egg-white dumplings over. Repeat with remaining egg-white mixture. When all dumplings are cooked, remove dumplings with a slotted spoon; place equal amounts in 4 serving bowls. Remove milk mixture from heat. In a medium bowl, beat egg yolks and 1/2 cup sugar with an electric mixer until pale and creamy, 5 to 7 minutes. Fold into milk mixture; simmer over low heat 5 minutes, stirring frequently. Add salt. Ladle milk mixture over dumplings. Lightly sprinkle with cinnamon. Serve hot or chilled. Makes 4 servings.

# Meat Broth

Wywar Miesny

*A basic, nourishing broth used in countless soups, sauces and main dishes.*

8 qts. water
8 to 9 lbs. meaty bones and meat scraps from beef, pork and veal, or a combination
2 medium onions, char-burned, see below
2 parsley roots, quartered
4 medium carrots, quartered
4 celery stalks, quartered
2 leeks
20 black peppercorns
2 tablespoons salt

Place water, bones and meat in a large stockpot. Cover; bring to a boil. Skim foam from surface until surface is clear. Reduce heat to medium. Cook, uncovered, 1 hour. Add onions, parsley roots, carrots, celery, leeks, peppercorns and salt. Cover; bring to a boil. Reduce heat to very low. Cover and simmer 3 hours. Strain broth into a large bowl. Discard meat scraps, bones and cooked vegetables. Cool broth, uncovered. Pour into quart or pint containers with tight-fitting lids. Refrigerate until fat congeals. Lift fat off with a fork; discard fat. Cover; refrigerate up to 2 days or freeze up to 3 months. Bring broth to a full boil before using. Makes about 5 quarts.

# Beef Broth

Wywar Wolowy

*Scraps of chicken and veal can be substituted for beef.*

4-1/2 qts. water
3-1/2 to 4 lbs. meaty bones and beef scraps
1 large onion, char-burned, see below
2 medium carrots, cut in 2-inch pieces
1 parsley root, quartered
1 leek
1 celery root, quartered
1/2 head Savoy cabbage, quartered
12 black peppercorns
Salt

Place water, bones and beef scraps in a stockpot. Bring to a boil over medium-high heat. Skim foam from surface until surface is clear. Reduce heat to medium. Cook, uncovered, 30 minutes. Add onion, carrots, parsley root, leek, celery root, cabbage and peppercorns. Reduce heat to low. Partially cover; simmer 2 to 2-1/2 hours. Season with salt to taste. Strain broth into a large bowl. Discard beef scraps, bones and cooked vegetables. Cool broth, uncovered. Pour into quart or pint containers with tight-fitting lids. Refrigerate until fat congeals. Lift fat off with a fork; discard fat. Cover; refrigerate up to 2 days or freeze up to 3 months. Bring broth to a full boil before using. Makes about 2-1/2 quarts.

*To char-burn an onion using a gas stove, hold peeled onion over the open flame using metal tongs until slightly charred. With an electric stove, place onions under the broiler, or halve them and burn the flat sides in an old frying pan.*

# Chicken Broth

Wywar z Kury

*Excellent alone or as a light, richly flavored base for other soups.*

1 (3-1/2-lb.) chicken, cut up
About 3 qts. water
3 large onions, halved
1 large onion, char-burned, page 27
1 leek
1 celery root, halved

1 parsley root, halved
1 head Savoy cabbage, quartered
4 allspice berries
2 teaspoons salt
8 black peppercorns

Place chicken and enough water to cover in a stockpot. Bring to a boil over high heat. Skim foam from surface until surface is clear. Reduce heat to medium-low; add remaining ingredients. Cook, partially covered, 2 to 2-1/2 hours. Strain broth into a large bowl. Discard cooked vegetables. Remove chicken meat from bones; reserve for other use. Discard bones and skin. Cool broth, uncovered. Pour into quart or pint containers with tight-fitting lids. Refrigerate until fat congeals. Lift fat off with a fork; discard fat. Cover; refrigerate up to 2 days or freeze up to 3 months. Bring broth to a full boil before using. Makes about 2 quarts.

# Vegetable Broth

Wywar z Warzyw

*This light, nourishing broth is served frequently during religious holidays.*

2 tablespoons butter or margarine
2 medium onions, chopped
4 qts. water
3 medium carrots, sliced
2 parsley roots, sliced
2 celery roots, sliced
1 leek

2 small celery stalks including leaves
1/2 head Savoy cabbage, quartered
2 tablespoons chopped fresh dill or
   1 tablespoon dill weed
15 black peppercorns
Salt

Melt butter or margarine in a medium skillet. Add onions; sauté over medium heat until tender. In a large stockpot, combine sautéed onions, water, carrots, parsley roots, celery roots, leek, celery stalks and cabbage. Bring to a boil over high heat. Reduce heat to low. Add dill and peppercorns. Season with salt to taste. Partially cover; simmer 1 to 1-1/2 hours. Strain broth into a large bowl. Discard cooked vegetables. Cool broth, uncovered. Pour into quart or pint containers with tight-fitting lids. Refrigerate up to 2 days or freeze up to 3 months. Bring broth to a full boil before using. Makes about 2-1/2 quarts.

*Fat removed from poultry and other meat broth can be used as a flavorful skillet grease for frying or sautéing meat.*

# How to Make Broth

1/Strain broth into a large bowl. Discard meat scraps, bones and vegetables. Pour broth into quart or pint containers with tight-fitting lids.

2/Refrigerate broth until fat congeals. Lift fat off with a fork; discard fat. Cover and refrigerate up to 2 days or freeze up to 3 months.

# Veal Broth

Wywar z Cieleciny

*For maximum flavor, ask your butcher to cut veal bones in half to expose the marrow.*

| | |
|---|---|
| **3-1/2 to 4 lbs. meaty veal bones** | **4 medium carrots, halved** |
| **2-1/2 qts. water** | **1 medium onion** |
| **1 parsley root, halved** | **1/2 lb. green cabbage** |
| **2 leeks** | **8 black peppercorns** |
| **1 celery root, halved** | |

In a large stockpot, boil enough water to cover veal bones. Add veal bones; bring water back to boil. Drain; discard water. Add 2-1/2 quarts water. Cover; bring to a boil over medium heat. Skim foam from surface until surface is clear. Cook 30 minutes. Add parsley root, leeks, celery root, carrots, onion, cabbage and peppercorns. Bring mixture to a boil. Reduce heat and cover. Cook 1-1/2 hours. Simmer, uncovered, 10 minutes. Strain broth into a large bowl; reserve veal for other use. Discard cooked vegetables. Cool broth, uncovered. Pour into quart or pint containers with tight-fitting lids. Refrigerate until fat congeals. Lift fat off with a fork; discard fat. Cover; refrigerate up to 2 days or freeze up to 3 months. Bring broth to a full boil before using. Makes about 2 quarts.

# Dried-Mushroom Soup     Photo on pages 126 & 127.

Barszcz Grzybowy

*For a meatless Christmas Eve soup, substitute water for meat broth.*

3 cups water
2 oz. dried mushrooms
2 qts. Meat Broth, page 27, or bouillon
3 tablespoons butter or margarine
1 leek, minced
1 large carrot, grated
1 medium celery root, grated

2 medium onions, chopped
1 tablespoon vegetable oil
1 tablespoon all-purpose flour
Salt
Freshly ground black pepper
Chopped fresh parsley or dill
Polish Ravioli, page 82, if desired

In a medium saucepan, bring water to a boil. Cool slightly. Add mushrooms; cover with a tight-fitting lid and refrigerate overnight. Bring mushrooms to a boil, uncovered, over high heat. Reduce heat to low. Simmer 1 hour. Remove mushrooms from liquid and cool; reserve liquid. Chop cooked mushrooms; return to reserved liquid. Heat broth or bouillon in a large saucepan. Melt butter or margarine in a large skillet. Add leek, carrot, celery root and onions. Sauté over medium-low heat 10 to 15 minutes or until tender. Add sautéed vegetables to hot broth or bouillon. Simmer, partially covered, over low heat 1 hour. Strain liquid; discard sautéed vegetables. Add chopped cooked mushrooms and mushroom liquid to strained liquid. Bring to a boil over medium heat. Heat oil in a small skillet. Stir in flour over medium heat until golden. Ladle 1 cup broth from soup into cooked flour mixture. Stir to combine. Return resulting mixture to soup. Bring to a boil, stirring constantly. Season with salt and pepper to taste. Serve hot, over Ravioli, if desired. Garnish with parsley or dill. Makes 6 to 8 servings.

# Fresh-Mushroom Soup

Zupa Pieczarkowa

*Each variety of edible mushroom lends its own unique flavor to this soup.*

2 tablespoons butter or margarine
1 lb. fresh mushrooms, thinly sliced
1 qt. Meat Broth, page 27, or bouillon
1 tablespoon Maggi seasoning
1 teaspoon sugar

Salt
Ground white pepper
1 tablespoon all-purpose flour
3/4 cup dairy sour cream
Chopped fresh parsley

Melt butter or margarine in a large skillet. Add mushrooms; sauté over medium heat until tender. Heat broth or bouillon in a medium saucepan; add sautéed mushrooms. Bring to a boil. Cover with a tight-fitting lid; simmer over low heat 15 minutes. Add Maggi seasoning and sugar. Season with salt and white pepper to taste. In a small bowl, combine flour and sour cream until smooth. Stir 1 cup hot broth into sour-cream mixture until smooth. Add sour-cream mixture to soup. Bring to a simmer, stirring constantly; do not boil. Ladle steaming soup into serving bowls. Garnish with parsley. Makes 4 servings.

# Onion Soup

Zupa Cebulowa

*For flavorful variations, substitute Gouda or other cheeses for the mozzarella.*

Cheese Grzanki, see below
2 lbs. onions (about 10 medium onions)
3 tablespoons butter or margarine
2 qts. Veal Broth, page 29, or bouillon
Salt

1/4 cup white wine
Sugar
8 thin slices mozzarella cheese
Ground sweet paprika

*Cheese Grzanki:*
8 slices slightly stale French bread
2 tablespoons butter or margarine,
   room temperature

Parmesan cheese
Ground sweet paprika

Prepare Cheese Grzanki. Halve onions lengthwise, then slice thinly. Melt butter or margarine in a large skillet. Add onions; sauté over medium heat 15 minutes or until onions turn a light golden color. Heat broth or bouillon in a large saucepan. Add sautéed onions. Season with salt to taste. Bring to a boil. Reduce heat to low. Simmer 30 minutes, uncovered. Add wine and sugar to taste if onions are not sweet enough. Ladle soup into ovenproof serving bowls. Place 1 Cheese Grzanki on top of soup in each bowl. Top Cheese Grzanki with 1 slice cheese. Sprinkle cheese with paprika. Place filled serving bowls under broiler. Broil 5 minutes or until cheese melts and begins to brown. Makes 8 servings.

**Cheese Grzanki:**
Preheat oven broiler. Butter both sides of bread slices; arrange on a baking sheet. Sprinkle Parmesan cheese and paprika over bread slices. Broil 3 to 5 minutes or until golden brown.

# Potato Soup

Zupa Ziemniaczana

*For variety, use chicken, veal, beef or pork broth.*

6 medium potatoes, peeled, cut into
   1/2-inch cubes
2 medium carrots, thinly sliced
2 celery stalks, thinly sliced
1 medium onion, chopped
1-1/2 qts. water
2 cups Meat Broth, page 27, or bouillon

2 tablespoons butter or margarine
2 tablespoons all-purpose flour
1/2 teaspoon salt
1/4 teaspoon ground white pepper
1 cup milk
Chopped fresh parsley

Place potatoes, carrots, celery and onion in a large saucepan. Add water and broth or bouillon. Cover with a tight-fitting lid. Cook over medium heat 30 minutes or until vegetables are tender. In a small saucepan, melt butter or margarine. Stir in flour, salt and white pepper. Cook over medium heat, stirring constantly until mixture bubbles. Slowly add 1/4 cup milk, stirring until smooth. Add remaining milk, stirring until smooth. Bring to a boil, stirring constantly. Stir into hot broth mixture. Bring to a simmer over medium heat. Reduce heat to low and simmer 10 minutes. Serve hot, garnished with parsley. Makes 6 to 8 servings.

# How to Make Kohlrabi Soup

1/Root vegetables are common in Polish cooking. Vegetables, right to left, are leek, kohlrabi, celery root and parsley root.

2/Rub about 1/2 the cooked kohlrabi through a sieve. Add to kohlrabi stock. Discard remaining cooked kohlrabi.

# Barley-Vegetable Soup

Krupnik

*A soup that takes the chill out of winter evenings.*

**1/4 cup butter or margarine**
**1 medium carrot, sliced**
**1 leek, sliced**
**1 celery stalk, sliced**
**1 small onion, chopped**
**1/4 cup barley grits**
**2 qts. Meat Broth, page 27, or bouillon**

**2 bay leaves**
**4 black peppercorns**
**1 teaspoon salt**
**4 large dried mushrooms**
**4 medium potatoes, peeled, diced**
**Chopped fresh parsley**

Melt butter or margarine in a large skillet over medium heat. Add carrot, leek, celery, onion and barley. Cook, uncovered, 10 to 12 minutes, stirring several times. In a large saucepan, bring broth or bouillon to a boil. Add cooked vegetables, bay leaves, peppercorns and salt. Cover; bring to a boil. Reduce heat to low; cook 30 minutes. Wash and chop dried mushrooms. Add mushrooms and potatoes to broth or bouillon mixture. Cover and simmer over low heat 30 minutes or until potatoes are tender. Remove and discard bay leaves. Ladle hot soup into serving bowls. Garnish with parsley. Makes 6 to 8 servings.

# Kohlrabi Soup

Zupa z Kalarepy

*Kohlrabi is not a cabbage or a turnip, yet in many ways resembles both.*

1-1/2 qts. water
About 1 lb. young kohlrabi, peeled,
   quartered
1/2 celery root, halved
1 parsley root, halved
2 leeks, white only
2 tablespoons butter or margarine
1 tablespoon all-purpose flour

1 qt. Meat Broth, page 27, or bouillon
2 egg yolks
1 cup half and half
Salt
Sugar
1/4 cup chopped fresh dill
Cheese Grzanki, if desired, page 31

Heat water in a large saucepan. Add kohlrabi, celery root, parsley root and leeks. Cook, covered, over medium-low heat 30 minutes or until vegetables are tender. Strain resulting stock into a large saucepan; discard celery root, parsley root and leeks. Rub about 1/2 of kohlrabi through a sieve into kohlrabi stock. Discard remaining kohlrabi. In a small skillet, melt 1 tablespoon butter or margarine. Add flour; stir over medium heat until smooth. When flour mixture starts to bubble, stir in 1 cup broth or bouillon. Stir thinned flour mixture into kohlrabi stock. Add remaining broth or bouillon. Bring to a boil. Remove from heat. In a medium bowl, combine egg yolks and half and half. Pour egg-yolk mixture into hot soup, stirring rapidly. Add remaining 1 tablespoon butter or margarine. Season with salt and sugar to taste. Add dill and Cheese Grzanki, if desired. Makes 8 to 10 servings.

# Cauliflower Soup

Zupa Kalafiorowa

*Homemade String Noodles add just the right touch to this light and tangy soup.*

String Noodles, page 70
1 medium cauliflower
1 pint water
2 qts. Veal Broth, page 29, or bouillon
1/2 pint dairy sour cream (1 cup)

3 tablespoons all-purpose flour
1 teaspoon sugar
Salt
Chopped fresh parsley

Prepare String Noodles. Wash cauliflower; separate flowerets. Cut into 1-inch pieces. In a medium saucepan, place cauliflower and water. Cook over high heat, uncovered, 20 minutes or until cauliflower is tender and water evaporates. In a large saucepan, bring broth or bouillon to a boil. Add cauliflower. In a small bowl, combine sour cream and flour until smooth. Stir 1 cup hot broth or bouillon into flour mixture. Stir resulting mixture into soup. Add sugar. Season with salt to taste. Place String Noodles in serving bowls. Ladle steaming soup over noodles. Garnish with parsley. Makes 6 servings.

**Variation**

In a small bowl, combine 1/2 pint dairy sour cream (1 cup) with 3 egg yolks, instead of flour. Gently stir into soup before serving.

# Dill-Pickle Soup

Zupa Ogorkowa

*A favorite with pregnant Polish women — and expectant fathers as well.*

| | |
|---|---|
| 2-1/2 qts. water | 1/2 teaspoon salt |
| 2-1/2 lbs. pork spareribs | 3 medium potatoes, peeled, quartered, sliced |
| 2 medium carrots, sliced | 2 tablespoons butter or margarine |
| 1/2 celery root | 4 medium dill pickles, peeled, grated |
| 1 parsley root | 1 tablespoon all-purpose flour |
| 1 bay leaf | 1/2 cup dairy sour cream |
| 10 black peppercorns | Dill-pickle juice, if desired |

Place water and spareribs in a large saucepan. Bring to a boil over medium-high heat. Skim foam from surface until surface is clear. Cook, uncovered, 10 minutes. Add carrots, celery root, parsley root, bay leaf, peppercorns and salt. Reduce heat to medium-low. Cook, uncovered, 1 hour or until meat is tender. Remove meat and bones; reserve for other use. Add potatoes; cook 20 minutes or until tender. Melt butter or margarine in a small skillet. Add pickles; sauté over medium heat until tender, 8 to 10 minutes. Add to soup. Bring to a boil. Simmer, uncovered, over low heat 45 minutes. Remove celery root, parsley root and bay leaf; discard. In a small bowl, combine flour and sour cream until smooth. Stir 1 cup broth into sour-cream mixture until smooth. Return sour-cream mixture to soup. Simmer 5 minutes; do not boil. Serve hot. If soup is not sour enough, add dill-pickle juice to taste, if desired. Makes 6 servings.

# Fresh-Dill Soup     Photo on page 36.

Zupa Koperkowa

*A classic Polish soup, excellent with chicken, veal or rabbit.*

| | |
|---|---|
| String Noodles, page 70 | 2 tablespoons butter or margarine |
| 2 qts. Meat Broth, page 27; | 1 cup chopped fresh dill with |
|    Vegetable Broth, page 28; or |    no seeds or branches |
|    bouillon | Salt |

Prepare String Noodle batter. In a large saucepan, bring broth or bouillon to a boil. Drizzle noodle batter into boiling liquid with a spoon, a few drops at a time, while stirring gently. Melt butter or margarine in a small skillet. Add dill; sauté over medium heat 3 minutes or until almost tender. Do not brown. Stir dill into hot liquid. Simmer 5 minutes, covered, over low heat. Season with salt to taste. Makes 6 servings.

### Variations

Instead of String Noodles, add 1/2 cup cooked long-grain white rice.

**Potato-Dill Soup:** In a small bowl, combine 3/4 cup dairy sour cream and 3 tablespoons all-purpose flour until smooth. Add 1 cup broth or bouillon; blend. Stir sour-cream mixture into soup. Add about 2 cups diced, peeled, cooked small new potatoes.

# Fresh-Cabbage Soup

Zupa ze Swiezej Kapusty

*Prepare this fast, inexpensive, tasty soup when time is at a premium.*

**2 to 2-1/4 cups chopped fresh green cabbage**
**1 medium onion, chopped**
**1 pint water**
**1/2 cup dairy sour cream**
**1 tablespoon all-purpose flour**
**5 cups Chicken Broth, page 28;**
   **Veal Broth, page 29;**
   **Meat Broth, page 27; or bouillon**

**1 tablespoon Maggi seasoning**
**Salt**
**Pinch of ground white pepper**
**Chopped fresh parsley or dill**

Place cabbage, onion and water in a medium saucepan. Cook, uncovered, over medium heat 15 to 20 minutes or until tender. In a small bowl, combine sour cream and flour until smooth. Place broth or bouillon in a large saucepan. Bring to a boil. Stir 1 cup hot broth or bouillon into sour-cream mixture. Return mixture to saucepan. Bring to a boil, uncovered, over medium-high heat, stirring occasionally. Add cabbage mixture. Simmer, uncovered, over low heat 10 minutes. Add Maggi seasoning. Season with salt and white pepper to taste. Simmer 5 minutes. Serve steaming hot. Garnish with parsley or dill. Makes 6 servings.

# Sauerkraut Soup

Kapusniak

*For a milder flavor, rinse sauerkraut before using it.*

**1 lb. sauerkraut**
**1 (2- to 2-1/2-lb.) ham bone**
**6 black peppercorns**
**1 bay leaf**
**3 qts. water**

**6 medium potatoes, peeled, diced**
**1/4 lb. bacon, diced**
**2 medium onions, chopped**
**2 tablespoons all-purpose flour**

Place sauerkraut, ham bone, peppercorns, bay leaf and water in a stockpot. Cover; bring to a boil. Uncover; cook over medium heat 1-1/2 hours. In a medium saucepan, cook potatoes with enough water to cover until tender; drain well. Add potatoes to sauerkraut mixture. In a small skillet, sauté bacon over medium heat until crisp. Remove bacon and drain on paper towels. Reserve 2 tablespoons bacon drippings. Add bacon to sauerkraut mixture. In reserved drippings, sauté onions stirring until golden brown. Stir in flour. Ladle 1 cup sauerkraut broth into onion mixture; stir to combine. Stir resulting mixture into soup. Bring to a boil. Remove and discard bay leaf. Serve hot. Makes 10 servings.

*After lending their unique flavors to broth, firm root vegetables, such as carrots, parsley root and celery root, can be diced and included in mixed-vegetable side dishes.*

# Cold Cucumber-Beet Soup

Chlodnik

*A refreshing chilled soup you can prepare for hot summer days.*

1 lb. small beets with greens
   (8 to 10 beets)
2 qts. Beef Broth, page 27, or
   bouillon
2 tablespoons lemon juice or vinegar
1 pint dairy sour cream, sour milk or
   buttermilk (2 cups)

2 medium cucumbers, peeled, thinly sliced
6 radishes, thinly sliced
2 tablespoons chopped fresh dill or
   1 tablespoon dill weed
1 tablespoon chopped chives
1 teaspoon salt
3 hard-cooked eggs, thinly sliced or chopped

Scrub beets; rinse beet greens. Peel, then slice beets; chop beet greens. In a large saucepan, combine sliced beets, chopped greens, broth or bouillon, and lemon juice or vinegar. Cover with a tight-fitting lid. Bring to a boil over high heat. Reduce heat to low; simmer, partially covered, 30 minutes or until tender. Strain liquid into a large bowl; reserve beets and beet greens. Let strained liquid cool. To cooled liquid, add sour cream, sour milk or buttermilk. Beat with an electric mixer until frothy, 2 to 3 minutes. Add cooked beets, beet greens, cucumbers, radishes, dill, chives and salt. Refrigerate 1 hour. Garnish with sliced or chopped hard-cooked eggs. Serve chilled. Makes 6 to 8 servings.

### Variations

Add 1 cup chopped cooked veal.
Add 10 medium shrimp, shelled, deveined, cooked, diced.
Add 2 thinly sliced dill pickles.

# Borscht

Barszcz

*This is one of the most traditional Polish soups.*

1-1/2 lbs. fresh beets
1 tablespoon salt
2 qts. Meat Broth or
   Beef Broth, page 27; or bouillon
2 tablespoons vinegar

Pinch of freshly ground black pepper
Lemon juice
Sugar
Chopped fresh dill or parsley

Scrub and rinse beets clean; rinse with cold water. Leave roots, 1 to 2 inches stem, and skin intact. Place whole washed beets in a large saucepan. Add salt and enough cold water to cover. Bring to a boil over high heat. Cover with a tight-fitting lid; reduce heat to medium-low. Cook 1 hour or until tender. Remove beets from liquid. Let cool, then peel. Heat broth or bouillon in a large saucepan. Slice or grate cooked beets; add to broth or bouillon. Simmer, uncovered, over low heat 30 minutes. Stir vinegar and pepper into beet mixture. Season with lemon juice and sugar to taste. Simmer over low heat 1 hour; do not boil. Strain into a serving tureen. Serve steaming hot. Garnish with dill or parsley. Makes 6 servings.

### Variation

**Christmas Eve Borscht:** Photo on pages 126 & 127. Substitute Vegetable Broth, page 28, for broth or bouillon. Add 1 tablespoon vegetable oil. Serve hot over Mushroom-Filled Ravioli, page 83.

Top to bottom: Tripe Soup, page 38; Cold Cucumber-Beet Soup, above; and Fresh-Dill Soup, page 34, with String Noodles, page 70, and Soup Crackers, page 41.

# Tripe Soup    Photo on page 36.

Flaki

*A recipe well worth the effort, and a favorite of native Poles.*

3-1/2 lbs. beef tripe
Water
2 carrots
1 parsley root
1 leek
3 small onions
4 celery stalks
1 medium leek, white only
1/4 cup butter or margarine
1/3 cup grated parsley root

1/2 cup grated carrot
1-1/2 qts. Beef Broth, page 27, or
    bouillon
5 black peppercorns
1/2 teaspoon salt
1/8 teaspoon ground marjoram
1/8 teaspoon ground nutmeg
1 tablespoon Maggi seasoning
2 tablespoons all-purpose flour

In a large stockpot, place tripe; cover with water. Bring to a boil and boil 5 minutes. Discard water. Rinse tripe with cold water. In same stockpot, place 3 quarts water, cooked tripe, 2 carrots, 1 parsley root, 1 leek, 2 small onions and 2 celery stalks. Cover; cook over medium heat 3-1/2 hours. Remove tripe; let cool. Discard cooking liquid and cooked vegetables. Cut tripe, remaining leek and celery into thin strips, 1/4 inch wide and 1 to 1-1/2 inches long. Quarter and slice remaining onion into strips. In a medium skillet, melt 2 tablespoons butter or margarine. Add leek strips, onion strips and celery strips. Add grated parsley root and grated carrot. Sauté over medium heat about 5 minutes. Add 1/4 cup water. Cover and cook over medium heat 10 minutes, stirring several times. In a large saucepan, place broth or bouillon. Add tripe, cooked vegetables and peppercorns. Bring to a boil. Reduce heat to low. Add salt, marjoram, nutmeg and Maggi seasoning. In a small skillet, melt remaining 2 tablespoons butter or margarine. Stir in flour; stir over medium heat until golden. Ladle 1 cup broth into cooked flour mixture. Stir to combine. Return resulting mixture to soup. Bring soup to a boil. Serve hot. Makes about 6 servings.

# Fish Soup

Zupa Rybna

*Most freshwater fish can be used in this basic recipe.*

Fish Croquettes, page 114
2 lbs. fresh fish, dressed
2 qts. water
2 medium carrots, quartered
2 medium onions

6 black peppercorns
1 bay leaf
3 allspice berries
Salt
Thin lemon slices

Prepare Fish Croquettes. In a large stockpot, combine fish, water, carrots, onions, peppercorns, bay leaf and allspice. Simmer, uncovered, over low heat 30 minutes or until fish is easily removed from bones. Strain into a large bowl, reserving broth; discard solids. Add Fish Croquettes to broth. Season with salt to taste. Simmer over low heat 5 minutes. Serve garnished with lemon slices. Makes 4 to 6 servings.

# How to Make Tripe Soup

1/In a large stockpot, combine water, cooked tripe, carrots, parsley root, leek, onions and celery. Cover and cook.

2/Cut tripe, leek and celery into thin strips. Sauté vegetables over medium heat about 5 minutes.

# Farmer's Vegetable Soup

Gospodarska Zupa Warzywna

*Use this delicious, nutritiously balanced soup as a main dish.*

**2 qts. Meat Broth, page 27, or bouillon**
**1/3 cup cut fresh green beans**
**1/3 cup cut fresh yellow beans**
**1/2 celery root, diced**
**1/3 cup sliced carrot**
**1/3 cup kohlrabi, cut into 1/2-inch cubes**
**1/2 cup chopped green cabbage**
**2 parsley roots or 1 large bunch**
   **parsley sprigs tied together**

**2 bay leaves**
**10 black peppercorns**
**1 cup diced, peeled, new potatoes**
**1/3 cup fresh or frozen green peas**
**1/2 cup fresh or frozen whole-kernel corn**
**1/2 pint dairy sour cream (1 cup)**
**2 tablespoons all-purpose flour**
**Salt**

Heat broth or bouillon in a stockpot. Add green beans, yellow beans, celery root, carrot, kohlrabi, cabbage, parsley roots or parsley, bay leaves and peppercorns. Partially cover; cook over medium-low heat about 20 minutes. Add potatoes; cook over medium heat, partially covered, 20 minutes. Add peas and corn; cook 10 minutes or until vegetables are tender. In a medium bowl, combine sour cream and flour. Stir 1 cup hot broth into sour-cream mixture until smooth. Return sour-cream mixture to soup; stir to blend. Season with salt to taste. Remove and discard bay leaves and parsley sprig bunch, if used. Serve hot. Makes 8 to 10 servings.

# Yellow-Pea Soup

Grochowka

*Smoked ham lends a distinctive flavor to this nourishing dish.*

| | |
|---|---|
| Ham Broth, see below | 2 oz. bacon, diced |
| 1 cup dried yellow split peas | 1/4 cup minced onion |
| 1 qt. water | 1 tablespoon all-purpose flour |
| 4 medium potatoes, peeled, diced | Chopped fresh parsley |

*Ham Broth:*

| | |
|---|---|
| 2 to 2-1/2 lbs. smoked ham with bone | 10 black peppercorns |
| 3 celery stalks | 1 bay leaf |
| 4 medium carrots, quartered | 1 teaspoon salt |
| 1 parsley root | 3 qts. water |
| 1 leek | |

Prepare Ham Broth. In a medium saucepan, combine split peas and 1 quart water. Cover with a tight-fitting lid. Bring to a boil. Reduce heat to low; simmer 2 hours or until peas are tender. Drain peas in a fine-mesh metal strainer; discard liquid. Pour Ham Broth into a large saucepan. Using the back of a wooden spoon, mash peas through strainer into broth. Ladle broth through strainer until only hulls remain in strainer. Add potatoes to broth. Bring to a boil. Cook over medium heat, uncovered, 20 minutes or until potatoes are tender. In a small skillet, sauté bacon over medium heat until crisp. Add onion; cook until tender. Stir flour into bacon and onion. Cook over medium heat, stirring until flour becomes golden, 2 to 3 minutes. Ladle 1 cup broth into bacon mixture. Stir to blend in flour. Combine resulting mixture with soup. Bring to a boil. Serve hot. Garnish with parsley. Makes 6 to 8 servings.

**Ham Broth:**
Place all ingredients in a stockpot. Cover with a tight-fitting lid. Simmer over low heat 2-1/2 hours. Strain; reserve ham for other use. Discard vegetables.

# Tomato Soup

Zupa Pomidorowa

*Of all Polish soups, this is my favorite.*

| | |
|---|---|
| 3 tablespoons butter or margarine | 3 tablespoons all-purpose flour |
| 4 lbs. ripe tomatoes, quartered | 1/2 pint dairy sour cream (1 cup) |
| (about 16 medium tomatoes) or | 1 tablespoon sugar |
| 1 (6-oz.) can tomato paste | Salt |
| 2 qts. Chicken Broth, page 28; Meat Broth, | Chopped fresh parsley or dill |
| page 27; or bouillon | |

Melt butter or margarine in a large skillet. Add tomatoes; cover and cook over medium heat, stirring occasionally, 20 minutes or until skins shrivel. Pour tomatoes into a fine-mesh strainer. With a wooden spoon, press tomatoes through strainer into a large bowl, mashing pulp and liquid through strainer. Discard tomato skins and seeds. Place broth or bouillon in a large saucepan. Bring to a boil over medium heat. Add strained tomatoes or tomato paste. In a small bowl, combine flour and sour cream. Stir 1 cup tomato mixture into flour mixture. Then return mixture to saucepan. Stir into tomato mixture until smooth. Add sugar. Season with salt to taste. Simmer over low heat 5 minutes. Serve hot. Garnish with parsley or dill. Makes 8 to 10 servings.

# Soup Crackers   Photo on page 36.

Groszek Ptysiowy

*Prepare these tiny crackers in advance for ease at serving time.*

| | |
|---|---|
| 1/4 cup water | About 1 cup all-purpose flour |
| 3 tablespoons butter or margarine | 1 egg, beaten |

Combine water and butter or margarine in a small skillet. Bring to a boil over medium heat. After butter or margarine melts, reduce heat to low. Slowly add 1 cup flour, stirring until mixture comes away from bottom and side of skillet, and resembles coarse meal. Remove from heat. Let cool. Preheat oven to 425F (220C). Grease a baking sheet. Add egg to flour mixture. Using your hands, work egg into flour mixture; knead into a smooth dough. If dough is too moist and sticky, add a little flour. Press dough into a ball. On a large lightly floured board, shape dough into a 1-inch-diameter rope. Roll dough back and forth against the board, using both hands. Cut 1/4-inch-thick slices from dough. Roll each piece into a small ball. Place on greased baking sheet. Bake 15 to 20 minutes or until golden brown. Serve in hot soups or as a garnish. Makes about 72 crackers.

# Stick Crackers

Paluszki

*A tasty slender cracker, often served with onion soup or other hot soups.*

| | |
|---|---|
| 1/4 cup warm milk (110F, 45C) | 1 cup butter or margarine, melted, cooled |
| 1 teaspoon sugar | 1/2 teaspoon salt |
| 1 (1/4-oz.) pkg. active dry yeast | 1 egg, beaten |
| (1 tablespoon) | Poppy, sesame or dill seeds |
| 2-1/2 cups all-purpose flour | |

Combine milk and sugar in a small bowl. Stir in yeast; let stand until foamy, 5 to 10 minutes. Place flour in a large bowl. Stir in yeast mixture. Add butter or margarine and salt. Work into a soft dough. Turn out dough on a lightly floured surface. Clean and grease bowl. Knead dough 6 to 8 minutes or until smooth and elastic, adding a little flour if dough is too soft. Place dough in greased bowl. Cover with a slightly damp towel. Let rise in a warm place, free from drafts, until doubled in bulk, about 1 hour. Grease 2 large baking sheets. Punch down dough; knead 1 minute. Divide dough into 4 equal parts. Cover 3 parts with a damp towel. Roll remaining part into a 1-inch diameter rope. Cut crosswise into 1-inch pieces. Roll out cut pieces into strips 5 to 6 inches long. Arrange on greased baking sheets, stretching strips to 7 inches. Make sure strips are of a uniform thickness. Brush with beaten egg; sprinkle with poppy, sesame or dill seeds. Repeat with remaining dough. Let strips rise, uncovered, 20 minutes. Preheat oven to 325F (165C). Bake 20 to 30 minutes or until golden brown. Cool on racks. Makes about 50 crackers.

# SALADS

In Poland, you can't just walk into a grocery store any time of year and pick up two or three heads of lettuce. And you can't store lettuce—even with refrigeration—for more than a week or two. So, the only time Poles can use lettuce is when it's in season, picked from their own gardens.

When lettuce is available, it's prepared in refreshing dishes, such as Fisherman's Salad. This is a combination of chopped iceberg lettuce, fresh onions or chives, chopped hard-cooked eggs and black olives seasoned with lemon juice, dried-leaf Italian seasoning, salt and freshly ground black pepper.

Because there's not much of a lettuce season, other vegetables, raw and cooked, have taken up the slack. There's Tomato Salad, a dish eaten at least once a week in most homes, when tomatoes are in season. It's simply fresh tomato wedges with chopped or thinly sliced onions in vinegar, seasoned with salt and lots of black pepper, and garnished with chopped fresh parsley.

Other vegetables have salads named in their honor, including leek, radish and cucumber. Celery root and parsley root make an appearance here, too, as do sauerkraut and apples.

There's a lot of chopping, slicing and shredding of carrots, cucumbers, radishes and leeks. Cold beets are found in several creations, including, of course, Beet Salad. Cabbage is used raw and cooked, and includes the red, green and Savoy varieties.

For spreading on canapés, choose recipes such as Cheese & Leek Salad or Beet & Horseradish

## Summer Salad

Salatka Wiosenna

*In Poland, this salad is prepared only when lettuce is in season.*

| | |
|---|---|
| 1 head iceburg lettuce, cut in thin strips | 1 tablespoon lemon juice |
| 2 medium tomatoes, each cut in 8 wedges | 1 hard-cooked egg, cut in thin strips |
| 2 small kohlrabi, peeled, cut in julienne strips | 2 to 3 green onions, chopped |
| | Salt |
| 1/3 cup dairy sour cream | Freshly ground black pepper |

Combine all ingredients in a large bowl. Season with salt and pepper to taste. Makes 6 servings.

Relish, a powerful combination of shredded cooked beets with horseradish.

Cold Vegetable Salad is a must at Polish wedding and holiday celebrations. It's prepared from cooked parsley root, potatoes and carrots, combined with fresh apple, dill pickle and hard-cooked eggs. They're all blended together in a sauce of mustard and mayonnaise. Egg Salad and Chicken Salad round out party buffet tables.

Store-bought salad dressings aren't popular or readily available in Poland. Instead, salads are livened up with freshly squeezed lemon juice, vinegar, vegetable oil or olive oil and, at times, with sour cream. Chopped fresh or dried parsley and dill greens are always there for garnish.

# How to Make Red-Cabbage Salad

1/Place cabbage in a large salad bowl. Add onion, apples, lemon juice and oil; toss. Lemon juice will bring red color back in cabbage.

2/To complete salad, arrange parsley sprigs around inner edge of bowl. Place egg wedges around salad. Serve chilled.

## Red-Cabbage Salad    Photo on pages 126 & 127.

Salatka z Czerwonej Kapusty

*Apple adds its distinctive flavor to this colorful salad.*

**1 medium head red cabbage, shredded
    (about 8 cups)**
**1 medium onion, cup in strips**
**2 medium tart apples, peeled, grated**
**Juice of 1 lemon**
**2 tablespoons olive oil**

**1/2 teaspoon sugar**
**Salt**
**Freshly ground black pepper**
**Parsley sprigs**
**2 hard-cooked eggs, cut in wedges**

In a large saucepan, boil enough salted water to cover cabbage. Drop cabbage into boiling water. Cook 5 minutes over medium-high heat. Drain; let cool. Place cabbage in a large salad bowl. Add onion, apples, lemon juice and oil; toss. Season with sugar, and salt and pepper to taste. Gently toss. Arrange parsley around inner edge of bowl. Place egg wedges around salad. Cover and refrigerate until ready to serve. Makes 10 to 12 servings.

*Cabbage loses its red color during cooking. Lemon juice will bring bright red color back.*

# Cabbage Salad

Salatka z Kapusty

*This salad is often prepared during winter in Poland when other vegetables aren't available.*

1 small head Savoy cabbage, shredded
2 tart apples, peeled, shredded
2 tablespoons lemon juice
1 teaspoon salt
1/2 teaspoon sugar

1/4 cup olive oil
1/8 teaspoon freshly ground black pepper
1 medium dill pickle, thinly sliced
2 tablespoons chopped fresh dill or parsley

Place cabbage and apples in a large bowl. Sprinkle with lemon juice, salt, sugar, oil and pepper; toss lightly. Top with pickle slices and dill or parsley. Cover and refrigerate 30 minutes. Serve chilled. Makes 8 to 10 servings.

# Sauerkraut Salad

Salatka z Kiszonej Kapusty

*This salad is often served with pork entrées, especially during the winter.*

1 lb. sauerkraut, drained
2 medium carrots, shredded
2 medium onions, chopped
2 tablespoons olive oil

1 teaspoon sugar
1/4 teaspoon salt
1/8 teaspoon freshly ground black pepper

Place all ingredients in a medium bowl; mix lightly. Cover and refrigerate 30 minutes. Serve chilled. Makes 6 to 8 servings.

# Sauerkraut & Red-Onion Salad

Surowka z Kiszonej Kapusty i Czerwonej Cebuli

*Do not rinse sauerkraut if a sour flavor is desired.*

1-1/2 lbs. sauerkraut,
   rinsed once if desired
2 tablespoons sugar
1 large red onion, chopped

1/4 cup olive oil
1 teaspoon lemon juice
1 medium red onion, thinly sliced
2 tablespoons chopped fresh parsley

Combine sauerkraut, sugar, chopped onion and oil. Top with lemon juice, onion slices and parsley. Cover and refrigerate 30 minutes. Serve chilled. Makes 8 servings.

# Radish Salad

Salatka z Rzodkiewek

*Chopped dill makes an already zesty salad even better.*

| | |
|---|---|
| **1 lb. radishes, thinly sliced** | **1/2 teaspoon salt** |
| **2 green onions, sliced** | **Ground white pepper** |
| **1/2 cup dairy sour cream** | **Lettuce leaves** |
| **1 tablespoon chopped fresh dill** | **Dill sprigs** |

In a medium bowl, combine radishes, green onions, sour cream, chopped dill and salt. Season with white pepper to taste. Serve chilled on lettuce leaves. Garnish with dill. Makes 6 to 8 servings.

# Beet Salad

Salatka z Burakow

*This simple recipe is prepared year-round throughout Eastern Europe and Russia.*

| | |
|---|---|
| **2 tablespoons vegetable oil** | **Sugar** |
| **1 medium onion, chopped** | **Salt** |
| **1 lb. shredded cooked beets** | **Freshly ground black pepper** |
| **2 tablespoons vinegar or lemon juice** | |

Heat oil in a medium skillet. Add onion; sauté over medium heat until tender. Add beets and vinegar or lemon juice. Season with sugar, salt and pepper to taste. Gently stir over low heat 15 minutes or until heated through. Remove from heat. Let stand in skillet 15 minutes. Serve warm. Makes 4 to 6 servings.

# Beet & Horseradish Relish     Photo on pages 2 & 3.

Cwikla

*This tangy blend of flavors is especially savored during the Easter and Christmas holidays.*

| | |
|---|---|
| **1/2 lb. grated fresh cooked or canned beets** | **Pinch of sugar** |
| **1/2 lb. prepared horseradish** | **Pinch of freshly ground black pepper** |
| **2 tablespoons lemon juice** | **Salt** |

Combine beets, horseradish, lemon juice, sugar and pepper in a small bowl. Add salt to taste. Cover and refrigerate overnight. Serve chilled over cold meats, sausage or sandwiches. Makes about 2 cups.

# Celery-Root Salad

Salatka z Selera

*If you can't locate celery root, substitute parsley root or parsnips.*

5 to 6 young celery roots, peeled,
   cut in narrow strips
1 medium onion, minced
1/2 cup olive oil

1/3 cup vinegar
2 tablespoons chopped fresh dill
Salt

Combine celery roots and onion in a medium bowl. In a small bowl, combine oil, vinegar and dill. Season with salt to taste. Pour oil mixture over celery-root mixture. Toss evenly to coat. Cover and refrigerate 1 hour. Serve chilled. Makes 6 to 8 servings.

### Variations

Add 3 tart apples, peeled, cut in narrow strips.
Instead of cutting celery roots and apples in strips, shred them.

# Cottage-Cheese Salad

Salatka z Twarogu

*Small portions of this salad are often eaten for breakfast.*

12 oz. small-curd cottage cheese (1-1/2 cups)
12 radishes, thinly sliced
2 tablespoons chopped chives

1/2 teaspoon salt
1/8 teaspoon freshly ground black pepper

Combine all ingredients in a small bowl. Cover and refrigerate 1 hour. Serve chilled. Makes 4 to 6 servings.

# Cheese & Leek Salad

Salatka z Sera i Porow

*Serve this pleasant salad for breakfast over fresh bread or as a side dish at dinner.*

1 cup Mayonnaise, page 53, or
   other mayonnaise
1 lb. American cheese, shredded

1 leek, diced
2 tablespoons lemon juice
Salt

Combine all ingredients in a medium bowl. Season with salt to taste. Cover and refrigerate 30 minutes. Serve chilled. Makes 6 to 8 servings.

# How to Make Leek Salad

1/To prepare leeks, remove dark-green tops and root end. Quarter leeks lengthwise. Wash under running water. Coarsely chop cleaned leeks.

2/Place leek salad in a serving bowl. Top with chopped walnuts. Garnish with yogurt and leek rings, if desired. Serve chilled.

# Leek Salad

Salatka z Porow

*For variety, substitute flavored yogurt for plain yogurt.*

**2 large leeks, coarsely chopped**
**2 tart apples, peeled, grated**
**Juice of 1 lemon**
**1/2 cup plain yogurt**

**3 tablespoons milk**
**1/4 teaspoon salt**
**2 tablespoons chopped walnuts**
**Yogurt, leek rings, if desired**

Place leeks and apples in a medium bowl. Sprinkle with lemon juice. In a small bowl, combine yogurt, milk and salt. Gently stir into leek mixture. Top with chopped walnuts. Garnish with yogurt and leek rings, if desired. Cover and refrigerate until ready to serve. Makes 4 servings.

# Tomatoes & Cucumbers in Sour Cream

Pomidory i Ogorki w Smietanie

*Polish farmers say that cucumbers should be sliced from the flower end to prevent a bitter flavor.*

4 medium tomatoes, each cut in 8 wedges
1 medium cucumber, peeled, sliced
1 medium onion, chopped

1/2 cup dairy sour cream
1/2 teaspoon salt
1/8 teaspoon ground white pepper

Combine tomatoes, cucumber and onion in a medium bowl. In a small bowl, combine sour cream, salt and white pepper. Stir sour-cream mixture into tomato mixture until vegetables are evenly coated. Cover and refrigerate until ready to serve. Makes 4 to 6 servings.

# Cucumber Salad

Mizeria

*The Polish name for this salad shouldn't deceive you—it's not that hard to make.*

3 medium cucumbers, peeled, thinly sliced
1-1/2 teaspoons salt
1/2 pint dairy sour cream (1 cup)

1/8 teaspoon ground white pepper
1 tablespoon lemon juice
1 tablespoon chopped fresh dill

Place cucumber slices in a medium bowl. Add salt; mix lightly until salt adheres evenly to cucumber slices. Cover and refrigerate 1 hour. Drain juice from cucumber slices. In a small bowl, combine sour cream, white pepper, lemon juice and dill. Add to cucumber slices; gently mix. Cover and refrigerate until ready to serve. Makes 4 to 6 servings.

# Tomato Salad

Salatka Pomidorowa

*A popular salad enjoyed at many Polish dinner tables.*

4 medium tomatoes, each cut in 8 wedges
1 large onion, chopped
1/4 cup white vinegar
1 tablespoon vegetable oil

Salt
Freshly ground black pepper
1 teaspoon chopped fresh parsley,
  if desired

In a medium bowl, combine tomatoes, onion, vinegar and oil. Add salt and pepper to taste. Add parsley, if desired. Cover and refrigerate until ready to serve. Makes 4 to 6 servings.

# Summer Egg Salad

Wiosenna Salatka z Jaj

*Yogurt gives this fresh-tasting salad just the right texture.*

1/2 cup plain yogurt
3 tablespoons olive oil
1 tablespoon Dijon-style mustard
4 hard-cooked eggs, diced
2 small onions, diced
1 cup iceburg-lettuce strips

2 tablespoons lemon juice
1/2 teaspoon salt
1/2 teaspoon sugar
2 tablespoons chopped fresh parsley
2 tablespoons chopped chives

Combine yogurt, oil and mustard in a small bowl. Place eggs, onions and lettuce strips in a medium bowl; mix lightly. Sprinkle lemon juice, salt and sugar over egg mixture. Add yogurt mixture, parsley and chives. Mix lightly until combined. Cover and refrigerate 30 minutes. Serve chilled. Makes 4 to 6 servings.

# Fisherman's Salad

Salatka Rybaka

*A zesty creation that goes nicely with any fish or seafood.*

1 head iceburg lettuce, chopped
1 cup chopped green-onion tops or chives
2 hard-cooked eggs, chopped
8 large pitted black olives, chopped
Juice from 1 lemon

1 tablespoon olive oil
1 teaspoon dried Italian seasoning
Salt
Freshly ground black pepper

Combine ingredients in a large bowl. Season with salt and pepper to taste. Cover and refrigerate until ready to serve. Makes 6 servings.

# Chicken Salad

Salatka z Kury

*Serve this nutritious, versatile salad as a side dish on lettuce leaves or as a sandwich spread.*

3 cups diced cooked chicken
1 cup drained canned or
  thawed frozen green peas
1/2 cup diced radishes
3/4 cup Mayonnaise, page 53, or
  other mayonnaise

2 tablespoons lemon juice
1/2 teaspoon salt
1/4 teaspoon freshly ground black pepper
1/4 teaspoon ground sweet paprika

Place chicken, peas and radishes in a medium bowl. In a small bowl, stir together mayonnaise, lemon juice, salt, pepper and paprika. Stir mayonnaise mixture into chicken mixture until evenly distributed. Cover and refrigerate 30 minutes. Serve chilled. Makes 6 to 8 servings.

# Vegetable Salad    Photo on pages 2 & 3.

Salatka Warzywna

*A party dish savored during winter holidays and at Easter.*

1 parsley root, halved
3 medium potatoes
3 medium carrots, halved
1 large apple
4 small dill pickles
1 celery stalk
3 hard-cooked eggs, peeled

2/3 cup cooked green peas
5 tablespoons Mayonnaise, opposite,
  or other mayonnaise
1/4 teaspoon prepared mustard
1 teaspoon salt
Pinch of ground white pepper

In a large saucepan, place parsley root, potatoes and carrots; add water to cover. Cover and cook over medium heat 30 minutes or until tender. Drain vegetables, discarding cooking liquid. Cool; cover and refrigerate cooked vegetables overnight. Peel parsley root, potatoes, carrots, apple and pickles; cut in 1/4-inch cubes along with celery and 2 eggs. Place cubed ingredients in a large bowl. Stir in peas. In a small bowl, combine mayonnaise, mustard, salt and white pepper. Gently stir into vegetable mixture. Cover and refrigerate overnight. When ready to serve, slice remaining hard-cooked egg. Arrange slices on salad as garnish. Makes 8 to 10 servings.

**Variation**

Substitute 4 cups Meat Broth, page 27, for water when cooking vegetables.

# Herring Salad

Salatka Sledziowa

*Here's a lip-puckering version of a Polish-style herring salad full of tart flavors.*

1/2 lb. pickled herring, skinned,
  boned, chopped
1 medium dill pickle, peeled, chopped
1 tart apple, peeled, shredded
1/2 celery root, peeled, chopped
3 tablespoons Mayonnaise, opposite,
  or other mayonnaise

1 tablespoon dairy sour cream
1 tablespoon vinegar
Salt
Freshly ground black pepper
Half-slices of white or rye bread

In a medium bowl, combine pickled herring, dill pickle, apple and celery root. In a small bowl, combine mayonnaise, sour cream and vinegar. Gently stir into herring mixture. Season with salt and pepper to taste. Cover; refrigerate 1 hour. Serve chilled on half-slices of white or rye bread. Makes 10 to 12 servings.

# Fresh Garden Salad

Swieza Salatka

*This colorful salad will brighten up any dinner table.*

**3 medium tomatoes, each cut in 6 wedges**
**1 medium cucumber, peeled, thinly sliced**
**1 head iceberg lettuce, chopped**
**1 sweet red onion, thinly sliced**
**2 small sweet red peppers, chopped**

**1 tablespoon olive oil**
**Pinch of sugar**
**Salt**
**Freshly ground black pepper**

Combine tomatoes, cucumber, lettuce, onion, red peppers and oil in a large bowl. Season with sugar, salt and pepper to taste. Makes 8 servings.

**Variation**

Toss salad with 1/4 cup mayonnaise and 1 medium chopped dill pickle or sweet pickle.

# Buttered Bread Crumbs

Zarumieniona Bulka Tarta

*The simplest recipe in the book.*

**2 tablespoons dry bread crumbs**
**1 tablespoon butter or margarine**

Place bread crumbs in a small, dry skillet. Carefully cook over medium-high heat, stirring until golden. Do not burn. Remove from heat. Add butter or margarine; stir with a fork until melted. Serve warm, lightly spooning over vegetables, pierogies or noodles. Use sparingly. Makes enough to garnish 4 servings.

# Mayonnaise

Majonez

*A simple thick and creamy condiment that is more flavorful than commercial mayonnaise.*

**1 egg yolk**
**1 teaspoon dry mustard**
**1/2 teaspoon sugar**

**2 tablespoons lemon juice or vinegar**
**1/4 teaspoon salt**
**1 cup vegetable oil**

Place egg yolk, mustard, sugar, lemon juice or vinegar, and salt in a blender or food processor fitted with a metal blade; process until smooth. While continuing to blend, add oil, a few drops at a time, until all oil is blended in. Process until smooth. Mayonnaise should be thick and creamy. Pour into a small container. Cover tightly; refrigerate up to 1 week. Makes about 1 cup.

# VEGETABLES &

Throughout Polish culinary history, vegetables have had their ups and downs. The downs came centuries ago, when vegetables were considered something to be eaten only by peasants. In the 16th century, Polish King Sigmund I married the Queen of Italy. He brought his new wife, complete with cooks and attendants, to the Polish Court. To ease her cultural shock, the Queen imported a variety of her native Italian vegetables, mostly greens and tomatoes. At first the Queen was met with hearty laughs from Poles who remarked that "only Italians could get fat on vegetables."

But something went right, because vegetables took hold in the Polish Court and soon spread into the common Pole's diet. To this day, the Polish word for vegetables, *wloszczyzna,* means "Italian produce."

Many of the Polish cook's vegetables are grown in small backyard gardens. They are tilled by hand and watered at times with water cranked up from wells and hand-carried by children.

Beets, cabbage, cucumbers, tomatoes and onions are popular. Also common are asparagus, Brussels sprouts, the knoblike kohlrabi, carrots, green beans, green peas, dried beans and cauliflower.

Their table presentations are not fancy. Most vegetables are steamed or simmered in water or mixtures of sour cream, light cream or broth. Then they are garnished with bread crumbs sautéed in butter, chopped fresh parsley or dill, or presented in a simple sauce.

Some vegetables, such as tomatoes or cucumbers, are difficult to store, and can be used fresh only when in season. Onions, carrots, potatoes and other root vegetables are kept in earthen cellars through winter.

Introduced from Peru in the 16th century, potatoes took such firm root in Poland that today, more meals are served with them than without. Potatoes are mashed, baked, fried and rendered into the famous Potato Pancakes topped with an agreeable combination of cottage cheese and chopped chives. The Poles love pota-

## Beets

Buraki

*Select smooth, firm beets of uniform size for this popular side dish.*

**1-1/2 lbs. beets**
**1 tablespoon butter or margarine**
**1 tablespoon all-purpose flour**

**3 tablespoons dairy sour cream**
**1 tablespoon lemon juice**
**Salt**

Cut off beet stem ends. Scrub beets; rinse clean with cold running water. Place whole washed beets in a large saucepan. Add enough cold salted water to cover. Bring to a boil over high heat. Reduce heat to medium-low. Cover with a tight-fitting lid. Cook 1 hour or until fork-tender. Remove beets from cooking liquid; discard liquid. Let cool. Peel beets. Melt butter or margarine in a medium skillet. Shred beets into buttered skillet. Blend flour and sour cream in a small bowl. Gently stir sour-cream mixture and lemon juice into shredded beets. Season with salt to taste. Gently stir over medium-low heat until beets are hot. Serve immediately. Makes 6 servings.

# SAUCES

toes hollowed out and filled with stuffings made of cooked pork, sausage or beef, onions, hard-cooked eggs and sour cream. And the delicious, thinly sliced paprika-flavored Raw-Potato Home-fries begin many a Polish farm-worker's day.

Just as people in the West pick strawberries, blackberries and blueberries in the wilds, people in Poland gather mushrooms. In fact, most Polish children who live on farms or in small villages learn about wild mushrooms at a young age.

Mushrooms can be gathered only twice a year, so the Poles must resort to several methods of preserving them. They pickle small and button specimens. But pickling renders them useless for most recipes requiring the natural mushroom flavor. The most popular way to store and pre-serve mushrooms is to dry them. They are strung together so they're not touching one another, and hung in a place where there is constant low-heat temperature and plenty of circulating air. This is usually in the kitchen near the warm radi-ant stove, or by a window where both sunlight and gentle cooking heat provide slow dehydration. When dried, the mushrooms are stored for use later in countless soups, stews, salads, sauces or stuffings.

What can you say about sauces? The Polish sauce list reads like a who's who of Polish vegetables. There's Onion Sauce, Potato Sauce, Tomato Sauce and many more made with sour cream, sweet cream, wine and broth. Nothing fancy—nothing to keep the Polish cook from his or her other activities.

# Brussels Sprouts

Brukselka

*Serve your main meat surrounded by Brussels sprouts with this tasty sauce.*

**About 1 lb. Brussels sprouts**
**1 teaspoon sugar**
**1/4 cup milk**
**1 teaspoon chopped fresh dill**

**Dill Sauce with Sour Cream, below**
**1/4 cup dry bread crumbs**
**2 tablespoons butter or margarine**

Remove any wilted or yellow leaves from Brussels sprouts. Trim stems with a sharp knife, making a shallow cut in the bottom of each stem to promote even cooking. Rinse in cold water. Place in a medium saucepan. Add salted water to cover, sugar, milk and dill. Cover and simmer 10 to 15 minutes or until almost tender. While sprouts are cooking, prepare Dill Sauce with Sour Cream. Drain sprouts. Place in a heated serving dish; keep warm. Place bread crumbs in a small dry skillet. Stir over medium heat until golden brown. Remove from heat. Stir in butter or margarine until combined. Spoon browned bread crumbs over Brussels sprouts. Drizzle warm Dill Sauce over bread crumbs. Serve hot. Makes 4 servings.

# Dill Sauce with Sour Cream

Sos Koperkowy

*Serve this basic dill sauce over roast pork, beef or veal.*

**2 tablespoons butter or margarine**
**2 tablespoons all-purpose flour**
**1 cup Meat Broth, page 27, or bouillon**

**3/4 cup dairy sour cream**
**3 tablespoons chopped fresh dill**
**Salt**

Melt butter or margarine in a small skillet; stir in flour. Cook over medium heat until mixture bubbles. Blend in broth or bouillon; bring to a boil, stirring constantly, until thickened. Stir in sour cream and dill. Season with salt to taste. Serve warm. Makes about 1-3/4 cups.

Chicken with Mushroom Stuffing, page 89, surrounded by Brussels Sprouts and Dill Sauce with Sour Cream.

# Mushroom Casserole

Zapiekanka Pieczarkowa

*In Poland, this tasty dish is popular on meatless Fridays.*

1/4 cup butter or margarine
1 lb. fresh mushrooms, sliced
4 cups cooked noodles
4 eggs, beaten

1 teaspoon salt
1/4 teaspoon freshly ground black pepper
1/4 cup grated sharp Cheddar cheese (1 oz.)
2 tablespoons chopped fresh parsley

Melt 2 tablespoons butter or margarine in a large skillet. Add mushrooms; sauté over medium heat until tender. Place sautéed mushrooms in a medium bowl; set aside. Melt remaining butter or margarine in large skillet. Add noodles. Sauté over medium heat until lightly browned. Drizzle eggs over noodles. Add salt and pepper. Stir noodle mixture over medium heat until eggs are set. Reduce heat to low. Sprinkle cheese over noodle mixture. Add cooked mushrooms. Gently stir until heated through. Garnish with parsley. Serve immediately. Makes 6 servings.

# Mushrooms with Cream

Pieczarki w Smietanie

*This delightful side dish will complement fish or poultry entrées.*

1 tablespoon butter or margarine
1 lb. fresh mushrooms, sliced
1 small onion, chopped
1/4 cup water

1/8 teaspoon salt
Pinch of freshly ground black pepper
1 tablespoon all-purpose flour
1 cup half and half

Melt butter or margarine in a medium skillet. Add mushrooms, onion and water. Cover with a tight-fitting lid. Cook over low heat 25 minutes or until mushrooms are tender, stirring occasionally. Season with salt and pepper. In a small bowl, blend flour and half and half. Stir into mushroom mixture. Cook, uncovered, over medium heat, stirring frequently, until mixture thickens. Serve hot. Makes 4 servings.

# Carrots in Sauce

Marchewka w Sosie

*During winter, families in Poland store carrots in dark root cellars.*

Béchamel Sauce, page 69
10 medium-large carrots
About 1-1/2 cups water

1/2 teaspoon salt
1/2 teaspoon sugar
Chopped fresh parsley

Prepare Béchamel Sauce. Cut carrots into 1-1/2-inch-long pieces. With a sharp knife, split pieces lengthwise into wedges no wider than 3/8 inch. Place carrots, water to cover, salt and sugar in a large saucepan. Cover with a tight-fitting lid. Bring to a boil; cook over medium heat 25 minutes or until tender. With a slotted spoon, carefully remove carrots from liquid. Place carrots in a deep casserole or serving dish. Stir carrot juice into Béchamel Sauce. Bring to a simmer. Immediately pour over carrots. Garnish with parsley. Serve hot. Makes 8 to 10 servings.

# Tender Cabbage

Kapusta Zasamazana

*This old-time vegetable is as popular today as it was centuries ago.*

2 cups Meat Broth, page 27;
  Chicken Broth, page 28; or bouillon
1 (2-lb.) head Savoy or green cabbage,
  shredded
1 large carrot, shredded
2 tablespoons butter or margarine

1 onion, chopped
1-1/2 teaspoons all-purpose flour
2 tablespoons lemon juice or vinegar
1 teaspoon salt
1/8 teaspoon freshly ground black pepper
1 teaspoon sugar

In a large saucepan, combine broth or bouillon, cabbage and carrot. Cover and simmer 30 minutes. Melt 1 tablespoon butter or margarine in a small skillet. Add onion; sauté over medium heat until tender. Stir onion into cabbage mixture. Melt remaining butter or margarine in small skillet. Add flour; stir over medium heat until flour becomes golden brown. Stir 1/2 cup simmering broth into flour mixture. Add to cabbage mixture. Simmer 15 minutes, stirring frequently. Stir lemon juice or vinegar into cabbage mixture. Season with salt, pepper and sugar. Serve hot. Makes 8 servings.

# Asparagus

Szparagi

*Select thin young spears for this quick and delicious recipe.*

2 lbs. fresh asparagus
1/2 teaspoon sugar
1/4 cup dry bread crumbs

2 tablespoons butter or margarine
1 tablespoon lemon juice

Rinse asparagus in cold water. With your fingers, snap off hard ends; discard. In a large skillet, bring 1/2 inch salted water to a boil. Add asparagus and sugar. Cover with a tight-fitting lid. Bring to a boil. Reduce heat to medium-low. Cook 7 minutes or until crisp-tender; do not overcook. Drain and place on a warmed serving dish; keep warm. Place bread crumbs in a small dry skillet. Stir over medium heat until golden brown. Stir butter or margarine into bread crumbs until combined. Stir lemon juice into browned bread-crumb mixture. Spoon bread-crumb mixture over asparagus. Serve hot. Makes 6 servings.

**Variation**

Spoon bread crumbs over asparagus. Drizzle 1 cup Béchamel Sauce, page 69, over bread crumbs. Top with 1/4 cup grated Gouda or Parmesan cheese. Broil 3 to 4 minutes or until cheese melts and browns.

# How to Make Stuffed Cucumbers and Tomatoes

1/Fill cucumber shells with egg mixture. In a small bowl, combine flour and sour cream. Stir dill into sour-cream mixture. Spoon sour-cream mixture over filled cucumber shells.

2/Slice bottoms off tomatoes; discard bottoms. With a spoon, scoop out pulp, leaving a 3/4-inch shell. Stuff tomato shells with meat mixture.

# Stuffed Tomatoes

Nadziewane Pomidory

*Fresh, firm home-grown tomatoes are best for this dish.*

**3 tablespoons butter or margarine**
**1/2 lb. fresh mushrooms, minced**
**2-1/2 cups cooked ground pork, beef or veal**
**2 eggs, beaten**
**1/2 cup dry bread crumbs**

**2 tablespoons chopped fresh dill**
**1/2 teaspoon salt**
**1/8 teaspoon freshly ground black pepper**
**1/8 teaspoon ground nutmeg**
**6 medium-large ripe tomatoes**

Preheat oven to 350F (175C). Lightly grease an 8-inch-square baking dish. Melt butter or margarine in a large skillet. Add mushrooms; sauté over medium heat until tender. Add cooked pork, beef or veal; sauté 5 minutes or until meat is heated through, stirring over medium heat. Stir in eggs, bread crumbs, dill, salt, pepper and nutmeg. Slice **bottoms** off tomatoes; discard bottoms. With a spoon, scoop out pulp, leaving a 3/4-inch shell. Stuff tomato shells with meat mixture. Arrange stuffed tomatoes in greased baking dish. Pour water around tomatoes to a depth of 1/4 inch. Bake, uncovered, 15 minutes or until top of meat mixture browns. Serve immediately. Makes 6 servings.

# Stuffed Cucumbers

Ogorki Nadziewane

*This unusual method of preparing cucumbers will surprise and delight your dinner guests.*

4 small to medium cucumbers, peeled
2 tablespoons butter or margarine,
   room temperature
2 eggs, separated
2 tablespoons dry bread crumbs
1/2 teaspoon salt

1 tablespoon chopped fresh parsley
2 tablespoons water
1 teaspoon all-purpose flour
1/2 cup dairy sour cream
1 tablespoon chopped fresh dill

Cut 1/4 off each cucumber lengthwise. Use a spoon to scoop out seeds and pulp, leaving a 1/4- to 1/2-inch-thick shell. Preheat oven to 350F (175C). Heavily butter a medium baking dish; add 2 tablespoons water to baking dish. In a medium bowl, combine butter or margarine and egg yolks. Stir bread crumbs, salt and parsley into egg-yolk mixture. In a medium bowl, beat egg whites until stiff peaks form. Fold beaten egg whites into egg-yolk mixture. Fill cucumber shells with egg mixture. In a small bowl, combine flour and sour cream. Stir dill into sour-cream mixture. Spoon sour-cream mixture over filled cucumber shells. Arrange filled cucumber shells in baking dish. Bake, covered, 20 minutes or until tender when pierced with a fork. Serve hot. Makes 4 servings.

# Stuffed Green Peppers

Paprika Faszerowana

*Topped with steaming Tomato Sauce, these nutritious peppers make a fine entree.*

Tomato Sauce, page 68
4 large green bell peppers
1 tablespoon butter or margarine
1 medium onion, chopped
1/2 lb. ground beef or pork
2 tablespoons cooked long-grain white rice

1 egg, beaten
1 teaspoon salt
1/4 teaspoon freshly ground black pepper
2 medium tomatoes
1 cup Beef Broth, page 27;
   Veal Broth, page 29; or bouillon

Prepare Tomato Sauce. Preheat oven to 350F (175C). Lightly grease a shallow baking dish. Slice tops off peppers; dice edible parts of cut tops. With a spoon, scoop out seeds and pith; discard. Melt butter or margarine in a small skillet. Add diced green pepper and onion; sauté over medium heat until tender. Let cool. Combine ground beef or pork, rice and sautéed green pepper and onion in a medium bowl. Add egg, salt and black pepper. Stuff pepper shells with ground-meat mixture. Halve tomatoes vertically. Place 1/2 tomato, cut-side down, on top of each stuffed pepper. Arrange stuffed peppers in greased baking dish. Pour broth or bouillon in bottom of baking dish. Bake, covered, 45 minutes or until fork-tender. Serve hot with Tomato Sauce. Makes 4 servings.

# Potato Pancakes

Placki Kartoflane

*May also be served topped with Hungarian Goulash, page 128.*

**Cottage-Cheese Topping, see below**
**7 large new potatoes, peeled**
  **(about 3 lbs.)**
**1 medium onion**
**1 egg, beaten**

**3 tablespoons all-purpose flour**
**3/4 teaspoon salt**
**1/8 teaspoon freshly ground black pepper**
**Vegetable oil**

*Cottage-Cheese Topping:*
**12 oz. cottage cheese (1-1/2 cups)**
**1/4 cup chopped chives**

Prepare Cottage-Cheese Topping. Preheat oven to 350F (175C). Using a hand grater or food processor fitted with a shredding blade, shred potatoes to make about 4-1/2 cups. Squeeze potatoes to remove any liquid, reserving liquid in a small bowl. Place potatoes in a large bowl. Depending on age and type of potatoes used, up to 1 cup juice may be obtained. Finely grate onion. Stir together shredded potatoes, onion, egg, flour, salt and pepper. Discard top portion of reserved potato juice, leaving juice about 1/2 inch deep or about 1/4 cup. This bottom juice contains potato starch. Stir juice into potato mixture. In a large skillet, heat about 3 tablespoons oil. Drop 1 heaping tablespoon potato mixture into skillet. Smooth out into a pancake 2-1/2 to 3 inches round. Place as many as possible in skillet. Cook over medium-high heat until browned and crisp on bottom, about 3 minutes. Turn and cook other side until brown and crisp. Remove from skillet and drain on paper towels. When drained, transfer to a heat-proof serving plate; keep hot in a warm oven. Add oil to skillet as necessary. Serve hot with Cottage-Cheese Topping. Makes 35 to 40 pancakes.

**Cottage-Cheese Topping:**
In a small bowl, combine cottage cheese and chives.

# Raw-Potato Homefries

Ziemniaki Smazone

*For the tastiest homefries, use rich, aromatic paprika imported from Hungary.*

**1/4 cup butter or margarine**
**1 tablespoon vegetable oil**
**1 teaspoon ground sweet paprika**
**1/2 teaspoon salt**

**1/8 teaspoon freshly ground black pepper**
**2 medium onions, chopped**
**10 to 12 medium potatoes, peeled,**
  **thinly sliced**

Melt butter or margarine in a large skillet; stir in oil, paprika, salt and pepper. Add onions; sauté over low heat 3 to 4 minutes or until almost tender. Stir in potatoes. Increase heat to medium. Cover with a tight-fitting lid. Cook 20 minutes or until potatoes become tender, turning with a spatula several times. Remove lid. Increase heat to medium-high. Cook potatoes until crisp and browned on both sides, turning several times with a spatula. Serve hot. Makes 6 servings.

# How to Make Potato Cutlets

1/Place potato mixture on bread crumbs. Using your hands, shape potato mixture into a smooth log about 12 inches long. Roll log over in bread crumbs, pressing bread crumbs evenly into outer surface.

2/Slice potato log into 1-inch-thick pieces. Press remaining bread crumbs into cut sides of cutlets. Heat oil in a large skillet. Add cutlets; fry 5 minutes on each side or until both sides are browned.

# Potato Cutlets

Kotlety Ziemniaczane

*A fast, easy way to prepare potatoes to serve for any meal.*

**Mushroom Sauce, page 69**
**2 lbs. potatoes, boiled in skins, peeled**
**1 egg**

**1/4 cup all-purpose flour**
**1/2 cup dry bread crumbs**
**1/4 cup vegetable oil**

Prepare Mushroom Sauce. Grind, shred or mash boiled potatoes into a large bowl. Blend in egg and flour. Spread bread crumbs on a working surface. Using your hands, shape potato mixture into a smooth log about 12 inches long. Roll log over in bread crumbs, pressing bread crumbs evenly into outer surface. Slice potato log into 1-inch-thick pieces. Press remaining bread crumbs into cut sides of cutlets. Heat oil in a large skillet. Add cutlets; fry 5 minutes on each side or until both sides are browned. Serve immediately, topped with warm Mushroom Sauce. Makes 12 cutlets.

# Potato Surprise

Niespodzianka Ziemniaczana

*Select smooth, long potatoes of equal size.*

10 medium-large baking potatoes
1/4 cup butter or margarine
1 medium onion, chopped
2-1/2 cups ground cooked meat
1 egg, beaten
1 tablespoon chopped fresh parsley or
   1 teaspoon dry parsley flakes

1/2 teaspoon salt
1/8 teaspoon freshly ground black pepper
1 tablespoon ground sweet paprika
2 cups gravy or Mushroom Sauce, page 69,
   if desired

Cook potatoes in water to cover, over medium-high heat 15 minutes. Remove potatoes from water; discard water. Let potatoes cool; peel. Lengthwise, cut top 1/5 off each potato; reserve tops. Carefully hollow out each potato, leaving a 1/2-inch-thick shell; reserve potato flesh for other use. Preheat oven to 400F (205C). Grease a shallow baking dish. Melt 2 tablespoons butter or margarine in a medium skillet. Add onion; sauté over medium heat until tender. Blend in meat, egg, parsley, salt and pepper. Stuff potatoes with meat mixture; replace tops. Arrange potatoes in greased baking dish. Bake, uncovered, 15 minutes. Melt 2 tablespoons butter or margarine; stir in paprika. Brush mixture lightly over potatoes. Bake 45 minutes or until tender when pierced with a fork. Serve hot with gravy or Mushroom Sauce, if desired. Makes 10 servings.

# Stuffed Potatoes

Nadziewane Ziemniaki

*Reserve the potato flesh for making Raw-Potato Homefries, page 62.*

5 medium-large baking potatoes
3 tablespoons butter or margarine
1 medium onion, chopped
1 cup chopped, leftover, cooked lean beef,
   pork or sausage

1 hard-cooked egg, chopped
1 tablespoon dairy sour cream
Salt
Freshly ground black pepper

Scrub potatoes; pat dry with paper towels. Cut 1-1/2 inches off 1 end of each potato; reserve ends. Carefully hollow out each potato with a thin-bladed knife and spoon, leaving a 1/2-inch-thick potato shell. Reserve potato flesh for other use. Melt 1 tablespoon butter or margarine in a small skillet. Add onion; sauté over medium heat until tender. Preheat oven to 350F (175C). In a small bowl, combine sautéed onion, meat, egg and sour cream. Stuff potato shells with meat mixture. Recap potatoes by replacing ends; secure with wooden picks. Melt 2 tablespoons butter or margarine in a small skillet. Brush each potato with butter or margarine. Arrange potatoes on a rack in a baking dish. Bake 1 hour or until tender when pierced with a fork. To serve, slice lengthwise. Sprinkle with salt and pepper to taste. Makes 5 servings.

# How to Make Victory Rice

1/Evenly sprinkle bread crumbs over bottom of buttered baking dish. Spoon cooked rice over bread crumbs. Spoon peas over rice.

2/Scatter ham strips over peas. Season with salt and pepper. Pour eggs over ham. Sprinkle cheese on top of eggs.

# Victory Rice

Ryz Viktoria

*This dish is an excellent companion to Fresh-Dill Soup, page 34.*

**2 cups Chicken Broth, page 28;**
   **Beef Broth, page 27; or bouillon**
**1 cup uncooked long-grain white rice**
**1/2 cup dry bread crumbs**
**1 cup fresh or frozen green peas**

**1 lb. smoked ham, finely diced**
**Pinch of salt**
**Pinch of freshly ground black pepper**
**4 eggs, beaten**
**1 cup grated mild Cheddar cheese (4 oz.)**

Preheat oven to 300F (150C). In a medium saucepan, bring broth or bouillon to a boil. Add rice; cover with a tight-fitting lid. Cook over medium heat 10 minutes. Heavily butter bottom and sides of an 8-inch-square baking dish. Evenly sprinkle bread crumbs over bottom of baking dish. Spoon cooked rice over bread crumbs; smooth rice. Spoon peas over rice in an even layer. Slice ham into thin strips. Place on top of rice and peas. Season with salt and pepper. Pour eggs over ham. Sprinkle cheese on top of eggs. Bake, uncovered, 50 minutes or until lightly browned. Serve hot. Makes 4 to 6 servings.

# Horseradish Sauce

Sos Chrzanowy

*This sauce will spice up meat, fish, egg or casserole dishes.*

| | |
|---|---|
| **2 tablespoons butter or margarine** | **1 cup Meat Broth, page 27, or bouillon** |
| **1 tablespoon all-purpose flour** | **1/2 teaspoon lemon juice** |
| **1/2 pint dairy sour cream (1 cup)** | **1-1/2 teaspoons sugar** |
| **2 tablespoons prepared horseradish** | **Salt** |

Melt butter or margarine in a small skillet; stir in flour. Cook over medium heat until golden brown. Let cool. Stir cooled flour mixture into sour cream. Blend in horseradish. Heat broth or bouillon in a small saucepan. Add sour-cream mixture, lemon juice and sugar. Season with salt to taste. Remove from heat. Cool slightly. Serve warm. Makes about 2-1/4 cups.

### Variation

For a milder flavor, stir 2 beaten egg yolks into warm sauce.

# Cumberland Sauce

Sos Cumberland

*A little of this flavorful sweet sauce goes a long way.*

| | |
|---|---|
| **1 orange** | **1/4 cup apple juice or cider** |
| **5 tablespoons red wine** | **2 teaspoons prepared mustard** |
| **1/4 cup currant jelly** | |

Grate orange peel into a medium saucepan. Squeeze juice from orange; set aside. Add wine to peel; cook over medium heat 2 minutes. Add jelly, orange juice, apple juice or cider, and mustard. Beat with a wire whip until frothy. Pour into a small serving bowl. Serve over roast turkey or duck. Makes about 1-1/4 cups.

# Madeira Sauce

Sos Maderowy

*This sauce will turn inexpensive meat cuts into expensive-tasting dishes.*

| | |
|---|---|
| **3 tablespoons butter or margarine** | **2/3 cup Madeira wine** |
| **1-1/2 tablespoons all-purpose flour** | **1/2 teaspoon sugar** |
| **1 cup Meat Broth, page 27, or bouillon** | **Salt** |
| **1 tablespoon Maggi seasoning** | **Freshly ground black pepper** |

Melt butter or margarine in a small skillet. Stir in flour over medium heat until golden brown. Blend in broth or bouillon and Maggi seasoning. Simmer over low heat 15 to 20 minutes, stirring frequently. Add Madeira wine and sugar. Simmer over low heat 5 minutes, stirring constantly. Season with salt and pepper to taste. Serve hot. Makes about 1-3/4 cups.

# Potato Sauce

Sos Ziemniaczany

*The secret of this pleasant sauce is to not overcook the diced potatoes.*

**3 tablespoons butter or margarine**
**1 medium onion, diced**
**2 tablespoons all-purpose flour**
**1-3/4 cups Chicken Broth, page 28;**
**    Veal Broth, page 29; or bouillon**
**6 allspice berries**

**1 bay leaf, crushed**
**2 medium new potatoes, peeled, diced**
**1/2 tablespoon lemon juice**
**1/2 teaspoon salt**
**Pinch of ground white pepper**

Melt butter or margarine in a medium skillet. Add onion; cook over medium-low heat until tender. Stir in flour until smooth. Add broth, allspice and bay leaf. Simmer, uncovered, over low heat 15 minutes, stirring frequently. Strain cooking liquid into a small saucepan. Discard solids. Add potatoes to strained cooking liquid. Cook, uncovered, over medium-low heat, stirring occasionally 10 to 12 minutes or until potatoes are almost tender; do not overcook. Stir lemon juice into potato sauce. Season with salt and white pepper. Serve warm over hot kielbasa. Makes about 2 cups.

# Onion Sauce

Sos Cebulowy

*Serve over roast lamb or veal.*

**2 tablespoons butter or margarine**
**5 medium onions, finely chopped**
**1/2 cup Chicken Broth, page 28;**
**    Beef Broth, page 27; or bouillon**

**2 tablespoons all-purpose flour**
**1/2 cup half and half**
**1/2 teaspoon sugar**
**Salt**

Melt butter or margarine in a medium skillet. Add onions; sauté until tender. Using a spoon, press cooked onions and juices through a strainer into a medium bowl. Stir in broth or bouillon. In a small bowl, blend flour and half and half; stir into strained onion mixture. Add sugar. Return to skillet. Cook over low heat, stirring constantly, until mixture bubbles and thickens. Season with salt to taste. Serve warm. Makes about 1-1/2 cups.

# Tomato Sauce

Sos Pomidorowy

*Serve over hot sliced roast veal or pork.*

**1 cup Meat Broth, page 27, or bouillon**
**Béchamel Sauce, opposite**
**2 tablespoons tomato paste**

**1 teaspoon sugar**
**1/2 teaspoon ground sweet paprika**

Combine broth or bouillon, Béchamel Sauce and tomato paste in a medium saucepan. Stir in sugar and paprika. Cook over medium heat 5 minutes, stirring constantly. Makes 3 to 3-1/4 cups.

# Mushroom Sauce

Sos Pieczarkowy

*Excellent served over rice, noodles, potatoes or meat.*

2 tablespoons butter or margarine
1 lb. fresh mushrooms, thinly sliced
1 medium onion, chopped
2 tablespoons all-purpose flour
2 cups Chicken Broth, page 28;
   Beef Broth, page 27; or bouillon

1/4 teaspoon salt
1/4 teaspoon freshly ground black pepper
1/2 pint dairy sour cream (1 cup)

Melt butter or margarine in a large saucepan. Add mushrooms and onion. Cover with a tight-fitting lid; simmer over low heat 15 minutes, stirring occasionally. Stir flour into mushroom mixture until blended. Add broth or bouillon. Cover and simmer over low heat 30 minutes. Season with salt and pepper. Stir sour cream until blended; add to mushroom mixture, a little at a time, stirring until smooth. Cook over medium-low heat 2 minutes; do not boil. Serve hot. Makes about 4-1/2 cups.

# Béchamel Sauce

Sos Beszamelowy

*This recipe can be used to make a wide variety of other sauces.*

2 tablespoons butter or margarine
2-1/2 tablespoons all-purpose flour
1-3/4 cups milk
1/2 teaspoon salt

Pinch of ground white pepper
Pinch of ground nutmeg
1 tablespoon Maggi seasoning
Juice of 1 lemon

Melt butter or margarine in a medium saucepan. Stir in flour until smooth. Stir over low heat until bubbles begin to form. Gradually add milk, stirring constantly. Bring to a simmer. Stir in salt, white pepper, nutmeg and Maggi seasoning. Cook 5 to 7 minutes over medium heat until thickened. Stir lemon juice into sauce. Serve hot over meat, potatoes or vegetables. Makes about 2 cups.

# Mayonnaise Sauce

Sos Majonez

*This sauce is excellent over hot baked potatoes.*

1/2 cup shredded provolone cheese (2 oz.)
4 oz. cottage cheese (1/2 cup)
1 cup Mayonnaise, page 53, or
   other mayonnaise

1 tablespoon lemon juice
Chopped fresh parsley, if desired

In a blender or food processor fitted with a metal blade, blend provolone and cottage cheese. Add mayonnaise and lemon juice, processing until blended. Place in a small serving dish. Serve at room temperature. Garnish with parsley, if desired. Makes about 2 cups.

# PIEROGIES &

Of all Polish foods, none are more versatile than *pierogies*. From Polish, pierogi translates to "small pies" in English. But in any language, pierogies are a culinary delight, to be served as a main or side dish, snack or even as a dessert.

Pierogies have always been popular in Poland because they can be made with a seemingly endless variety of fillings, depending on what is available at the moment. With food supplies what they are in Poland, this comes in handy to the village housewives who must use all their resources to make the best of a poor situation.

If you've had pierogies before, you know how delicious they are. If you have yet to savor a pork, cheese or cabbage pierogi, you're in for a tasty surprise.

Contrary to popular belief, good pierogies are not difficult to make. Simple ingredients make up the dough, and the fillings are easily prepared using little more than a hand grinder.

When you begin making pierogies, a hand grinder is preferred over a blender or food processor because it is easier to control. Once you get a feel for the consistency that results from a hand grinder, you can switch to a more modern grinding method, if desired.

Here are a few helpful hints for pierogi-making.

For most pierogies, make dough *after* the savory filling has been prepared. However, when using a fruit filling, prepare dough first. That way, the juice won't be drawn out of the fruit prematurely while waiting for the dough to be completed. When boiling fruit pierogies, simmer them in water an additional 10 to 15 minutes.

All pierogies can be frozen for future use. You can dust unboiled pierogies with flour and freeze them in airtight containers. Or, place unboiled pierogies on baking sheets and freeze them 20 to 30 minutes. Then store them in plastic bags or other containers in a freezer. If you want to save time later, another alternative is to boil and drain pierogies, let them cool, and then freeze.

Most savory pierogies, especially pork, mushroom and cabbage, will benefit when sautéed with thinly sliced onions in butter. When serving, brush fruit pierogies with melted butter or softened cream cheese.

A close relative of the pierogi is the *uszka,* or "little ear." For all practical purposes, uszkas may be considered a Polish version of ravioli. These small filled dumplings are most commonly prepared with ground leftover cooked pork, beef or veal, mixed with bread crumbs and sautéed

## String Noodles
Photo on page 36.
Lane Kluski

*Simple-to-make no-fuss noodles.*

**2 eggs**
**1/4 cup all-purpose flour**

Beat eggs in a medium bowl. Stir in flour. Drizzle batter into boiling soup or broth while stirring gently. Batter will cook into noodles within the hot liquid in less than 1 minute. Makes enough noodles for 6 to 8 servings.

# DUMPLINGS

onions. Mushroom filling is popular for meatless holidays like Christmas Eve and certain days during Lent. Regardless of the filling, uszkas provide tasty additions to hot clear soups, or can be eaten by themselves, sautéed in butter like pierogies.

Another recipe that calls for fillings is *nalesniki*. Translated to "crepes," these thin rounds of cooked batter are made from eggs and flour. They can be rolled jelly-roll style or folded like pockets or envelopes around fillings of dry cottage cheese and chopped chives, or a zesty combination of chicken, mushrooms and onions.

*Kulebiak* means "fingers," but is prepared in a long roll that is sliced into individual serving pieces. Its filling consists of dried mushrooms, sauerkraut, onions and chopped hard-cooked eggs. Kulebiak can be served hot or cold.

Unfilled noodles include String Noodles, the batter of which is trickled into boiling broth or soup, and Round Dumplings, which are plain dumplings garnished with sautéed bread crumbs or crumbled crisp bacon.

# Potato Dumplings

Pyzy

*These dumplings can also be served with crumbled crisp-cooked bacon and sautéed onions.*

| | |
|---|---|
| **4 lbs. potatoes, peeled** | **1 teaspoon salt** |
| **Salt** | **1 egg** |
| **Water** | |

In a medium saucepan, place 1/3 of potatoes with enough salted water to cover. Bring to a boil over high heat. Reduce heat to medium. Partially cover; cook 20 minutes or until tender. Drain; let cool. Grind cooked potatoes into a large bowl; set aside. Grate remaining raw potatoes onto a piece of doubled cheesecloth about 20" x 12". Gather ends of cheesecloth so grated potatoes are enveloped in a ball. Squeeze excess potato juice into a medium bowl by twisting cheesecloth ends. Reserve potato juice. Stir squeezed raw potatoes into cooked potatoes. Add 1 teaspoon salt and egg. Work mixture together 3 to 4 minutes. From reserved potato juices, spoon off all but bottom 2 tablespoons potato juice which contains potato starch. Stir bottom 2 tablespoons juice into potatoes. Boil salted water in a large pot. Using your hands, roll 1 heaping teaspoon potato mixture into a ball. Drop potato dumplings into boiling water. Boil until potatoes are cooked and dumplings float, about 7 minutes. Makes 70 to 75 dumplings.

### Variation

**Stuffed Potato Dumplings:** Press 1 tablespoon potato mixture in your hand into a flat round. Place 1/2 teaspoon Meat Filling for Pierogies, page 81, in center. Roll potato mixture in a ball around filling. Cook as above. Makes 25 to 30 dumplings.

# Round Dumplings

Kluski Kladzione

*Excellent as leftovers the next morning, sautéed in butter.*

| | |
|---|---|
| **1 egg** | **1/8 teaspoon salt** |
| **2 tablespoons water** | **2 to 3 tablespoons buttered bread crumbs or** |
| **3/4 cup all-purpose flour** | **crumbled crisp-cooked bacon** |

Beat egg in a medium bowl. Add water; beat until smooth. Gradually add flour, beating constantly until smooth. Beat in salt. In a large stockpot, boil 5 to 6 inches of salted water. Dip a teaspoon in boiling water to prevent dough mixture from sticking to it. With the wet teaspoon, drop 1 scant teaspoon dough into boiling water. Dip spoon in water again; repeat process until all dough is used. Cover pot with a tight-fitting lid. Bring to a boil. Cook over medium-high heat 10 minutes or until all dumplings float. Watch carefully as liquid will easily boil over. Pour dumplings into a colander. Rinse with hot water. Garnish with bread crumbs or bacon. Serve hot with soups or as a side dish to meat. Makes 4 to 6 servings.

### Variation

Substitute 1/2 teaspoon onion salt for 1/8 teaspoon salt. Or, add 2 teaspoons minced onion or chives.

# Cheese-Filled Crepes

Nalesniki z Serem

*These light, nourishing creations are often served for breakfast.*

Cheese Filling, see below
3 eggs
1 cup water
1 cup milk

1-1/2 cups all-purpose flour
1/2 teaspoon salt
Butter or margarine

*Cheese Filling:*
1 lb. dry cottage cheese or
   ricotta cheese (2 cups)
1/2 cup chopped fresh chives
1 egg, beaten

1 egg yolk
Salt
White pepper

Prepare Cheese Filling. In a large bowl, beat eggs about 1 minute. Add water, milk, flour and salt. Beat into a smooth batter. Grease a crepe pan or 7-inch skillet with butter or margarine. Heat greased pan or skillet over medium heat. Pour a scant 1/4 cup batter onto center of hot pan or skillet. Tip skillet so batter is evenly distributed. Cook over medium heat until lightly golden. Turn and cook briefly until golden. Do not brown. Remove from skillet and place on a platter. Repeat process until all batter is used, greasing skillet as necessary. Fill and fold following one of the methods shown in photos, page 74. Melt 1 tablespoon butter or margarine in a large skillet. Place as many filled crepes as will fit in skillet without crowding. Cook over medium heat 3 to 4 minutes on each side or until both sides are golden. Place on a warm platter. Cook remaining crepes, adding butter or margarine as needed. Serve hot. Makes 16 to 18 crepes.

**Cheese Filling:**
In a grinder or food processor, grind cheese. Do not over process or puree. In a medium bowl, combine cheese, chives, egg and egg yolk. Season with salt and white pepper to taste.

**Variation**
**Sweet Cheese Filling:** Substitute 5 tablespoons sugar, 1 teaspoon melted butter or margarine and 1 tablespoon vanilla extract for chives, salt and pepper in above filling recipe.

# How to Fold Crepes

1/Method #1: Spread 1 tablespoon filling over inside 1/2 of a crepe. Roll crepe, filling-side first.

2/Method #2: Spread 1 tablespoon filling over inside 1/2 of a crepe. Fold crepe in half, then in half again.

3/Method #3: Spread 1 tablespoon filling over center of crepe, leaving a 1-inch border. Fold 1/3 crepe over filling, then fold in other 1/3 crepe. Fold ends in forming a small packet.

4/Sauté crepes over medium heat about 3 minutes on each side or until evenly browned. Place on a warm serving platter. Garnish with parsley, if desired.

# Chicken & Mushroom Crepes

Nalesniki z Kury z Grzybami

*If you prefer, substitute chopped cooked pork or beef for chicken.*

**Chicken & Mushroom Filling, see below**
**Béchamel Sauce, page 69, if desired**
**2 cups all-purpose flour**
**1/2 teaspoon salt**
**1/2 teaspoon ground white pepper**
**1/4 teaspoon ground nutmeg**
**2 egg yolks**
**1 cup milk**

**3/4 cup water**
**2 teaspoons Maggi seasoning**
**3 egg whites**
**Butter or margarine**
**2 eggs**
**1 cup dry bread crumbs**
**Chopped fresh parsley, if desired**

*Chicken & Mushroom Filling:*
**3 tablespoons butter or margarine**
**1/2 lb. fresh mushrooms, chopped**
**1 medium onion, chopped**
**3 tablespoons water**

**2 cups diced cooked chicken**
**Salt**
**White pepper**

Prepare Chicken & Mushroom Filling. Prepare Béchamel Sauce, if desired. In a large bowl, combine flour, salt, white pepper and nutmeg. In a small bowl, combine egg yolks, milk, water and Maggi seasoning. Stir egg-yolk mixture into dry ingredients making a smooth batter. Beat at least 5 minutes. In a medium bowl, beat egg whites until stiff peaks form. Fold beaten egg whites into batter until evenly distributed. Grease a crepe pan or 7-inch skillet with butter or margarine. Heat greased pan or skillet over medium heat. Pour 1/3 cup batter into hot pan or skillet. Using a round bottom of a spoon, smooth out batter to a 7- or 8-inch circle. Cook over medium to medium-low heat about 2 minutes. Turn with a spatula. Cook 1 to 2 minutes on other side. Do not brown or over cook as they will lose their pliability. Remove from skillet; place on a platter. Repeat with remaining batter, adding butter or margarine as needed. Fill and fold crepes following one of the methods shown in the photos, opposite. Beat eggs in a shallow medium bowl until blended. Place bread crumbs in a pie plate. Dip filled crepes in beaten egg, then in bread crumbs, pressing crumbs evenly onto surface of crepes. Melt 1 to 2 tablespoons butter or margarine in a large skillet. Place as many filled crepes, seam-side down, as will fit in skillet without crowding. Cook over medium heat 3 to 4 minutes on each side or until both sides are golden. Place on a warm platter. Cook remaining crepes, adding butter or margarine as needed. Serve hot, with Béchamel Sauce, if desired. Garnish with parsley, if desired. Makes 10 to 12 crepes or 5 to 6 servings.

**Chicken & Mushroom Filling:**
Melt butter or margarine in a large skillet. Add mushrooms, onion and water. Sauté over medium heat until mushrooms and onion are tender. Stir chicken into mushroom mixture. Reduce heat to medium-low. Cook 10 minutes, stirring, or until mixture is heated through and lightly browned. Season with salt and white pepper to taste. Remove from heat; let cool.

**Variation**
Preheat oven to 375F (190C). Grease a large shallow baking dish. After sautéing crepes, arrange in greased baking dish. In a small bowl, combine 1 cup dairy sour cream, 2 tablespoons shredded sharp Cheddar cheese and 1/4 teaspoon curry powder. Bake, uncovered, 10 to 12 minutes or until sour-cream mixture has a dull sheen. Serve immediately.

# Kulebiak

Kulebiak

*This is a baked, rolled dough filled with a delicious mushroom-sauerkraut mixture.*

Kulebiak Filling, see below
2 (1/4-oz.) pkgs. active dry yeast
  (2 tablespoons)
1/4 cup warm water (110F, 45C)
1-1/2 teaspoons sugar
About 4 cups all-purpose flour

3/4 cup warm milk (110F, 45C)
1 tablespoon butter or margarine, melted
1/8 teaspoon salt
1/8 teaspoon ground nutmeg
2 eggs, slightly beaten
1 egg white, beaten

*Kulebiak Filling:*
1 oz. dried mushrooms
2 lbs. sauerkraut, drained
2 tablespoons butter or margarine
2 large onions, minced

3 hard-cooked eggs, chopped
Salt
Freshly ground black pepper

Prepare Kulebiak Filling. In a small bowl, dissolve yeast in warm water. Stir in sugar and 1 tablespoon flour. Let stand until foamy, 5 to 10 minutes. Beat in milk, butter or margarine, salt, nutmeg, eggs and 2 cups flour. Stir in enough remaining flour to make a soft dough. Turn out dough onto a lightly floured surface. Clean and grease bowl. Knead dough 8 to 10 minutes or until smooth and elastic. Place dough in greased bowl, turning to coat all sides. Cover with a damp cloth. Let rise in a warm place, free from drafts, until doubled in bulk. Preheat oven to 350F (175C). Grease a large baking sheet. Punch down dough. Divide dough in 1/2. On a lightly floured surface, roll out 1/2 the dough to 14" x 12-1/2". Spread 1/2 Kulebiak Filling over rolled dough, to 1 inch of edge. Roll dough lengthwise, jelly-roll style. Crimp ends closed by pinching them together. Tuck ends under. Carefully place filled Kulebiak on greased baking sheet. Repeat with remaining dough and filling. Pierce each Kulebiak with a fork to allow steam to escape. Brush filled Kulebiak with egg white. Bake 45 minutes or until golden brown. Let cool slightly. Cut in 3/4- to 1-inch slices. Makes 2 rolls.

## Kulebiak Filling:

Place mushrooms in a medium saucepan; add water to cover. Let stand 6 to 8 hours or overnight. Cook mushrooms in soaking water, covered, over medium-low heat 1 hour or until tender. Strain liquid into a small bowl; reserve liquid. Finely chop mushrooms. Place sauerkraut and mushroom liquid in a large saucepan. Cook, uncovered, over medium heat 10 minutes or until liquid evaporates, stirring occasionally. Melt butter or margarine in a large skillet. Add onions; sauté over medium heat until tender. Add sauerkraut, mushrooms and eggs. Season with salt and pepper to taste. Cook over medium heat 5 minutes. Let cool.

Kulebiak

# Pierogies

Pierogi

*For variety, make each batch of these "small pies" with two different fillings.*

**Pierogi Fillings, pages 78 to 81**
**4 cups all-purpose flour**
**2 eggs**
**5 tablespoons dairy sour cream**
**6 tablespoons vegetable oil**

**Pinch of salt**
**About 3/4 cup water**
**Sautéed onions, if desired, or melted butter**
**  or softened cream cheese**

Prepare choice of Pierogi Fillings. Lightly flour 2 baking sheets. Sift flour into a large bowl or onto a flat working surface; make a well in the center. Break eggs into well. Add sour cream, 3 tablespoons oil and salt. Blend ingredients with your fingertips. Gradually add water, working and kneading mixture into a smooth, pliable dough. Divide dough into quarters. Cover 3 portions with a damp cloth. On a lightly floured board, roll 1 dough portion into a 1/16-inch-thick rectangle. Cut into 3-1/2 to 4-inch circles. In center of 1 dough circle, place 1 heaping tablespoon filling. Fold dough in 1/2 over filling. Crimp resulting edge with your fingertips, forming a tight seal. Repeat process until remaining dough is used, placing pierogies on lightly floured baking sheet. Bring a large saucepan of salted water to a boil, using 1/2 teaspoon salt per 2 quarts water. Drop about 5 pierogies into boiling water. Stir gently to prevent them from sticking to the bottom. When water returns to a boil, add 5 more pierogies. Stir carefully. Cover with a tight-fitting lid. Cook savory pierogies over medium heat, 4 to 5 minutes or until they float. Cook fruit pierogies 10 to 15 minutes. Gently remove pierogies from pot; drain in a colander or strainer. Rinse with hot water. Repeat until all pierogies are boiled. Pat dry with paper towels. For savory pierogies, heat remaining 3 tablespoons oil in a large skillet. Add 10 boiled pierogies; sauté over medium heat until browned on both sides, 5 to 6 minutes. Place in a large ovenproof serving dish. Keep hot in oven. Sauté remaining pierogies. Serve hot, garnished with sautéed onions, if desired. Serve boiled fruit pierogies brushed with melted butter or softened cream cheese. Makes about 70.

# Blueberry Filling for Pierogies

Nadzienie z Czarnych Jagod

*Use fresh blueberries for this delicious filling.*

**4 cups fresh blueberries**
**3 teaspoons sugar**

Wash berries; drain. In a medium bowl, sprinkle berries with sugar. Mix lightly. Fill pierogi shells immediately, before juice is drawn out of fruit. Makes about 4 cups or enough to fill 40 to 45 pierogies.

**Variation**

Substitute 4 cups blackberries, raspberries or sliced strawberries for blueberries.

# How to Make Pierogies with Cherry Filling

1/Roll pierogi dough to 1/16 inch thick. Cut into 3-1/2- to 4-inch circles. In center of 1 dough circle, place a heaping tablespoon of filling. Fold dough in half, over filling. Pinch to seal.

2/Pierogies can be sealed in several ways. Top to bottom, include a twisted rope effect done with your fingertips, crimping the edge with a dinner fork, and pinching the edge sealed, similar to sealing pie pastry.

# Cherry Filling for Pierogies

Czeresniowe Nadzienie

*Use fresh sweet or tart cherries for this popular summer pierogi filling.*

**4-1/2 cups dark sweet or red tart cherries**
**1 teaspoon lemon juice, if sweet cherries**

**Sugar to taste, if red tart cherries**

Wash, drain and pit cherries. Lightly press cherries in a strainer or colander to remove some juice. Place cherries in a medium bowl. If sweet cherries are used, sprinkle with lemon juice. If tart cherries are used, add sugar. Fill pierogi shells immediately, before juice is drawn out of fruit. Makes about 4 cups or enough to fill 40 to 45 pierogies.

# Vanilla-Cheese Filling for Pierogies

Pierogi Waniliowe

*With this filling, pierogies can be used as either a main dish or dessert.*

**2 lbs. dry cottage cheese or ricotta cheese
   (4 cups)**
**1 egg yolk**
**1/4 cup seedless raisins**

**1 teaspoon vanilla extract**
**Pinch of salt**
**Sugar**

Using a grinder or food processor fitted with a metal blade, process cheese. Do not puree or process too fine. In a large bowl, combine cheese, egg yolk, raisins, vanilla and salt. Add sugar to taste. Makes about 4 cups or enough to fill 40 to 45 pierogies.

# Cheese Filling for Pierogies

Pierogi z Serem

*Polish farmers make their own cottage cheese from curdled milk.*

**2 lbs. dry cottage cheese or ricotta cheese
   (4 cups)**
**1 egg plus 2 egg yolks, beaten**

**1/2 teaspoon salt**
**Pinch of ground white pepper**

Using a grinder or food processor fitted with a metal blade, process cheese. Do not puree or process too fine. In a large bowl, combine cheese, egg and egg yolks, salt and white pepper. Stir to combine. Makes about 4 cups or enough to fill 40 to 45 pierogies.

**Variation**
**Sweet Cheese Filling:** Add 1/4 cup granulated sugar and omit pepper. Stir until smooth. Serve hot filled pierogies with whipped cream.

# Meat Filling for Pierogies

Pierogi z Miesem

*Pork is the most popular of all meat fillings in Poland.*

1 lb. ground cooked pork, lamb, veal or beef (about 4 cups)
2 tablespoons butter or margarine
1 medium onion, chopped

2 eggs, beaten
1/2 teaspoon salt
1/2 teaspoon freshly ground black pepper

Using a grinder or food processor fitted with a metal blade, process meat. Do not puree or process too fine. Melt butter or margarine in a large skillet. Add onion; sauté over medium heat until tender. Stir in meat and eggs. Sauté over medium heat about 5 minutes. Season with salt and pepper. Let cool. Makes about 4 cups or enough to fill 40 to 45 pierogies.

# Sauerkraut Filling for Pierogies     Photo on pages 126 & 127.

Pierogi z Kapusty Kwaszonej

*Sauerkraut pierogies are traditionally served as a Christmas Eve main dish.*

1 lb. sauerkraut
2 tablespoons butter or margarine
1 medium onion, chopped

Pinch of salt
Pinch of freshly ground black pepper

In a medium saucepan, place sauerkraut and enough water to cover. Simmer, uncovered, over low heat 30 minutes. Drain well. Using a grinder or food processor fitted with a metal blade, process sauerkraut. Do not puree or process too fine. Melt butter or margarine in a large skillet. Add onion; sauté over medium heat until tender. Blend in sauerkraut, salt and pepper. Let cool. Makes about 4 cups or enough to fill 40 to 45 pierogies.

# Fresh-Mushroom Filling for Pierogies

Pierogi z Pieczarkami

*Use this filling for other dishes besides pierogies.*

1/4 cup butter or margarine
2 lbs. fresh mushrooms, minced
2 medium onions, minced

1/4 cup dry bread crumbs
1/2 teaspoon salt
1/2 teaspoon freshly ground black pepper

Melt 2 tablespoons butter or margarine in a large skillet. Add mushrooms; sauté over low heat until tender, stirring occasionally. Place sautéed mushrooms in a medium bowl. Melt remaining 2 tablespoons butter or margarine in skillet. Add onions; sauté over medium heat until tender. Let cool. Stir in bread crumbs. Stir mixture into sautéed mushrooms. Season mixture with salt and pepper. Makes about 4 cups or enough to fill 40 to 45 pierogies.

# How to Make Polish Ravioli

1/On a lightly floured board, roll each piece of dough into a 1/16-inch-thick rectangle. Cut dough into 2-inch squares. Place about 1 teaspoon filling in center of each square.

2/Fold each square in half diagonally to form a triangle. Pinch edges together; crimp closed. Fold 2 corners of longest edge so they overlap. Press overlapping corners together and crimp.

# Polish Ravioli

Uszka

*Fill these miniature dumplings with almost anything you want.*

**Ravioli Fillings, opposite**
**2-1/2 cups all-purpose flour**
**1/8 teaspoon salt**

**1 tablespoon butter or margarine, chilled**
**1 cup boiling water**
**1 egg yolk, lightly beaten**

Prepare choice of Ravioli Fillings. In a medium bowl, combine flour and salt. Using a pastry blender or 2 knives, cut butter or margarine into flour until mixture resembles coarse crumbs. Pour boiling water over mixture. Blend with an electric mixer until smooth, at least 5 minutes. Let cool. Blend in egg yolk. Cover and refrigerate 1 hour or longer. Divide dough into 8 equal portions. On a lightly floured board, roll 1 piece of dough into a 1/16-inch-thick rectangle. Cut into 2-inch squares. Place about 1 teaspoon filling in center of each square. Fold each square in 1/2 diagonally to form a triangle. Pinch edges together; crimp closed. Fold 2 corners of longest edge so they overlap. Press overlapping corners together and crimp. Bring a large saucepan of salted water to a boil, using 1/2 teaspoon salt per 2 quarts water. Drop about 10 ravioli into boiling water. Stir gently to prevent them sticking to the bottom. When water returns to a boil, add 10 more ravioli. Depending on size of pot, after 40 to 60 ravioli have been added, cover with a tight-fitting lid; cook over medium-high heat 4 to 5 minutes. Remove with a slotted spoon. Serve like Pierogies, page 78, or serve in hot soup. Makes about 115 ravioli.

# Meat Filling for Ravioli

Uszka z Miesem

*Meat can be leftovers from pork, beef or veal roasts, or meat used in broth-making.*

**3 tablespoons butter or margarine**
**1 large onion, minced**
**1/2 lb. ground cooked meat (about 2 cups)**

**1/4 cup Meat Broth, page 27, or bouillon**
**1/4 cup dry bread crumbs**
**1 egg, lightly beaten**

Melt butter or margarine in a medium skillet. Add onion; sauté over medium heat 3 to 5 minutes or until tender. Add meat, broth or bouillon and bread crumbs. Cook, uncovered, over medium heat about 10 minutes, stirring constantly. Let cool. Blend in egg. Makes enough filling for about 115 ravioli.

# Mushroom Filling for Ravioli   Photo on pages 126 & 127.

Uszka z Grzybami

*For a delightfully different flavor, rehydrate dried mushrooms in red wine.*

**3 oz. dried mushrooms**
**2 tablespoons butter or margarine**
**3 medium onions, minced**
**3/4 teaspoon salt**

**1/4 teaspoon freshly ground black pepper**
**2 tablespoons dry bread crumbs**
**1 egg white, lightly beaten**

Place mushrooms in a medium bowl; add water to cover. Let stand 6 to 8 hours or overnight. Grind mushrooms in a hand grinder. Melt butter or margarine in a medium skillet. Add onions; sauté over medium heat 3 to 5 minutes or until tender. Add ground mushrooms, salt, pepper and bread crumbs. Cook, uncovered, over medium heat about 15 minutes, stirring constantly. Let cool. Blend in egg white. Makes enough filling for about 115 ravioli.

# POULTRY

If you visit Poland, you might be surprised at how often chicken is served in homes and restaurants. When most people think of Polish main dishes, they think of pierogies, stuffed cabbage, kielbasa or pork recipes. Although those dishes certainly are important, the true culinary workhorse of the Polish kitchen is the common chicken.

Polish housewives appreciate the fact that chicken is one of the most versatile meats available. Its nutritious, sweet, delicious meat can be breaded and fried, sautéed, roasted, stewed and used to make croquettes, patties and casseroles. Chicken can be enjoyed hot or cold, and its leftovers are welcome in any home.

During the two decades I lived in Poland, I can't remember my mother ever buying chickens at a grocery store. Like thousands of others who owned small farms or houses with tiny fenced-in yards, we raised our own.

Once each spring, my mother would hitch our horse and wagon and travel seven miles to town to pick up a wide, flat boxful of 70 to 80 chirping "peeps"—baby chicks that would eventually provide nourishing, delicious meat and eggs for our family throughout the year.

Families in Poland that don't raise their own birds depend on their poultry "know-how" when they purchase chicken for the table. Even in cities like Warsaw and Cracow, most chickens are bought live or freshly killed from neighboring village farmers, or in the countryside at one of the many farmer's markets that open for business at the crack of dawn.

Because chicken is relatively easy to obtain in Poland—compared with red meats—a large variety of chicken dishes exist. As mentioned earlier, Chicken Soup ranks number one on the popularity list. Chicken breasts are breaded and fried, or ground after cooking and made into patties or slender, bite-size Chicken Fingers, which are also breaded and fried. A favorite Sunday dish is roast chicken cooked with a delicious stuffing containing mushrooms cooked in wine.

Turkeys are not considered a staple in Poland.

## Chicken in Spicy Cream Sauce

Kura w Ostrym Sosie Smietanowym

*A tasty combination of chicken and cream spiced with garlic, paprika and lemon.*

**2 large garlic cloves, crushed**
**1 tablespoon salt**
**1/2 teaspoon ground sweet paprika**
**1 (3- to 3-1/2-lb.) chicken, quartered**

**3 tablespoons vegetable oil**
**1 cup half and half**
**2 tablespoons lemon juice**
**1 tablespoon chopped fresh parsley**

Combine garlic, salt and paprika in a small bowl. Rub chicken pieces with garlic mixture. Let stand 15 minutes. Heat oil in a large skillet. Add chicken; cook chicken over medium heat, 10 minutes on each side or until both sides are browned. Combine half and half and lemon juice in a small bowl; spoon over chicken. Cover and simmer 1 hour or until tender, turning once. Place chicken in a warm serving dish. Spoon hot cooking juices over chicken. Garnish with chopped parsley. Makes 4 servings.

# & EGGS

These big birds are sometimes stuffed, but usually are roasted for the holidays. They're rubbed with a mixture of oregano, paprika, cloves, salt and pepper, and stuffed with pieces of apple, celery, carrot and green pepper.

Although most Polish cooks rate the chicken before the egg on their popularity list, eggs nonetheless are close behind. They're indispensable for baking, and play major and minor roles in appetizers, soups, salads, vegetables and many other dishes. Indeed, you'll find eggs within every chapter of this book. Naturally, they also provide the ingredients from which light, nourishing main dishes are prepared.

Although the eggs Poles use in the cooking are neither uniform in size, color or even shape, one trait is characteristic of all. The eggs are deliciously fresh, gathered by children who go through the barn chasing hens off their nests, some of which are built high in lofts. On many occasions, in order to come up with the freshest egg, my youngest brother would hide near a nesting hen and patiently wait for the moment of truth.

The egg dish most often prepared in Poland is scrambled eggs cooked with chunks of smoked pork loin. It's to be eaten at breakfast with fresh rolls or bread spread with hard white butter.

But there are also omelets made with pieces of kielbasa, ham, mushrooms, peas, spinach and even herring. Like elsewhere, in Poland eggs are fried, soft-boiled, poached, and baked in little ramekins with cream and minced ham.

Eggs play an important role in traditional Easter celebrations in the Polish household. Eggs are colored fancily with the same beeswax and dye system made popular by the Ukrainians, or plainly, using onion skin, beet juice and wild-root dyes. Every Easter, godparents bring children baskets filled with candy, presents and colored eggs. The children make a contest of cracking colored egg against egg until only one—the winning egg—is left unscathed.

# Chicken Fingers

Paluszki z Kury

*These handsome tidbits will outdo any chicken finger-food you'll find in restaurants, wings down.*

**4 chicken-breast halves, skinned, boned**
**2 tablespoons ground sweet paprika**
**1 tablespoon salt**
**1 teaspoon freshly ground black pepper**

**About 1 cup dry bread crumbs**
**2 eggs**
**Vegetable oil**

Cut each chicken piece lengthwise in 5 equal strips. Place each chicken strip between plastic wrap. Using a meat mallet, pound chicken strips until about 1/4 inch thick. In a heavy plastic bag, combine paprika, salt and pepper. Add chicken strips; shake to coat evenly. Or, spread strips on a flat surface. Sprinkle evenly with paprika mixture. Arrange seasoned strips on a baking sheet. Let stand 15 minutes. Place bread crumbs in a shallow dish. In a small, shallow bowl, beat eggs. Dip seasoned chicken strips in eggs, then in bread crumbs. Pour oil 1/2 inch deep in a large skillet. Heat to 350F (175C) or until a 1-inch bread cube turns golden brown in 65 seconds. Fry coated chicken strips jn hot oil, until golden brown, 2 to 3 minutes turning once. Drain on paper towels. Serve hot. Makes 20 pieces or 4 servings.

# Vienna Chicken

Kurczak po Wiedensku

*Poles love the tasty flavor of fresh garlic offered in this simple dish—and so will you!*

**1 (4- to 4-1/2-lb.) chicken, skinned, boned**
**5 garlic cloves, minced**
**1 tablespoon salt**
**1/4 teaspoon freshly ground black pepper**
**2 eggs**
**1 tablespoon half and half,**
  **whipping cream or milk**

**1/2 cup all-purpose flour**
**About 1 cup dry bread crumbs**
**Vegetable oil**
**Butter or margarine, room temperature**
**Fresh parsley sprigs**

Cut chicken in serving-size pieces. Place chicken pieces between plastic wrap. Using a meat mallet, pound about 3 to 4 times on each side. Combine garlic, salt and pepper in a small bowl. Rub chicken all over with garlic mixture. Let stand 15 minutes. Place eggs and half and half, cream or milk in a small shallow bowl. Lightly beat with a fork. Place flour and bread crumbs in separate shallow dishes. Roll a chicken piece in flour, then dip in beaten egg and roll in bread crumbs. Press crumbs evenly onto chicken. Place coated chicken on a wire rack. Repeat with remaining pieces. Let stand 15 to 20 minutes at room temperature to firm coating. Or, refrigerate until ready to cook. Preheat broiler. Pour oil 1/4 inch deep in a large skillet. Heat oil. Add chicken; fry over medium heat 5 to 6 minutes or until both sides become golden brown, turning once. Drain on paper towels. Arrange fried chicken in a large shallow baking dish. Place a small dab of butter or margarine on each piece. Broil chicken 2 minutes. Garnish with parsley. Serve immediately. Makes 6 servings.

# How to Make Chicken Fingers

1/Cut each chicken piece lengthwise in 5 equal strips. Place each chicken strip between plastic wrap. Using a meat mallet, pound until about 1/4 inch thick.

2/Arrange seasoned chicken strips on a baking sheet. Let stand at room temperature 15 minutes. Dip seasoned chicken strips in eggs, then in bread crumbs.

---

# Chicken Roll with Vegetables

Kurcze z Jarzynami

*If you can't find parsley root, substitute a parsnip in the vegetable filling.*

**10 chicken-breast halves, skinned, boned**
**2 tablespoons butter or margarine**
**3 medium carrots, finely chopped**
**2 medium onions, finely chopped**
**1 parsley root, finely chopped**
**1-1/4 cups Chicken Broth, page 28, or**
   **bouillon**

**2 eggs, beaten**
**1/4 cup frozen or fresh cooked green peas**
**Salt**
**Freshly ground black pepper**

Place chicken-breast halves between plastic wrap. Using a meat mallet, pound until chicken is about 1/4 inch thick. Trim each chicken piece into a rectangular shape, cutting away about 1/4 meat. Finely chop trimmed meat. Melt butter or margarine in a large skillet. Add carrots, onions, parsley root and 1/4 cup broth or bouillon. Sauté over medium heat 15 minutes or until cooking juices are reduced to about 2 tablespoons. Reduce heat to low. Stir eggs and peas into vegetables. Simmer until eggs set, stirring constantly. Add chopped chicken. Season with salt and pepper to taste. Sauté 3 to 4 minutes. Remove from heat; let cool. Preheat oven to 325F (165C). Grease a 13" x 9" baking dish. Evenly spread cooked chicken mixture on flattened chicken-breast rectangles. Roll chicken pieces from short end, jelly-roll style. Secure with wooden picks. Place chicken in greased dish seam-side down. Pour 1 cup broth or bouillon over chicken. Cover and bake 40 to 50 minutes or until fork-tender. Makes 5 to 6 servings.

# Chicken in Flames

Kura w Plomieniach

*Prepare this dramatic dish for an intimate candlelight dinner.*

| | |
|---|---|
| 1 (3- to 3-1/2-lb.) chicken | 2 tablespoons strong Polish vodka or |
| 1 tablespoon salt | other vodka |
| Stuffing, see below | |

*Stuffing:*

| | |
|---|---|
| 4 stale dinner rolls | 1/4 cup dry bread crumbs |
| 1/2 cup milk | 1 tablespoon finely chopped walnuts |
| 1/4 cup butter or margarine | 1 tablespoon finely chopped almonds |
| 2 eggs | 1 teaspoon ground nutmeg |
| 1 teaspoon salt | 1/4 cup chopped fresh parsley |

Rub chicken, inside and out, with 1 tablespoon salt; let stand 15 minutes. Prepare Stuffing. Preheat oven to 375F (190C). Grease a deep baking dish. Fill chicken body cavity with stuffing. Place stuffed chicken in greased dish. Cover and bake 30 minutes. Remove cover; bake 30 minutes or until juices run clear when a knife is inserted between breast and thigh. Using a heavy cleaver or knife, cut chicken in quarters. Place chicken quarters, skin-side up, on a platter. Pour vodka over chicken. Using a long match, carefully ignite vodka. Serve immediately. Makes 4 servings.

**Stuffing:**
In a medium bowl, soak rolls in milk. In a food processor fitted with a metal blade, process soaked rolls, butter or margarine, eggs, salt, dry bread crumbs, walnuts, almonds, nutmeg and parsley.

# Baked Chicken with Mushrooms

Kura Pieczona z Pieczarkami

*The combination of sweet onions and tangy sour cream creates a special dinner treat.*

| | |
|---|---|
| 1 (3- to 3-1/2-lb.) chicken, cut up | 2 cups Chicken Broth, page 28, or |
| 1 teaspoon salt | bouillon |
| 1/4 cup all-purpose flour | 1/2 lb. fresh mushrooms, sliced |
| 4 tablespoons butter or margarine | 1 cup dairy sour cream |
| 1 teaspoon ground sweet paprika | 2 tablespoons chopped fresh parsley |
| 2 medium onions, chopped | |

Rub chicken pieces with salt; let stand 15 minutes. Preheat oven to 325F (165C). Grease a 13" x 9" baking dish. Place flour in a shallow dish. Roll chicken pieces in flour until evenly coated. Melt 3 tablespoons butter or margarine in a large skillet. Add floured chicken; sauté over medium heat until chicken browns on all sides. Arrange chicken in greased baking dish; reserve pan juices. Sprinkle paprika evenly over chicken. Add onions to skillet of cooking juices. Sauté over medium heat until tender. Spoon sautéed onions over chicken. Pour broth or bouillon over chicken. Cover and bake 45 minutes. Melt 1 tablespoon butter or margarine in a medium skillet. Add mushrooms; sauté over medium heat until tender. Spoon cooked mushrooms over chicken. Spoon sour cream over chicken. Garnish with parsley. Cover; bake 15 to 20 minutes or until chicken is tender. Makes 4 to 6 servings.

# Chicken with Mushroom Stuffing    Photo on page 57.

Kura z Pieczarkowym Nadzieniem

*Mushrooms cooked in white wine bring a wonderful flavor to this inexpensive dish.*

**Mushroom Stuffing, see below**
**1 (3- to 3-1/2-lb.) chicken**
**Salt**

**Ground sweet paprika**
**Freshly ground black pepper**
**Gravy, see below**

*Mushroom Stuffing:*
**2 cups white wine**
**3 tablespoons butter or margarine**
**1 lb. fresh mushrooms, sliced**
**1 chicken liver, minced**
**1 cup stale bread cubes or croutons**

**1/4 teaspoon freshly ground black pepper**
**1/4 teaspoon ground nutmeg**
**1/2 teaspoon salt**
**2 tablespoons chopped fresh parsley**
**2 eggs, beaten**

*Gravy:*
**1 tablespoon Maggi seasoning**
**1/2 cup white wine**
**1 cup Chicken Broth, page 28, or bouillon**

**1 tablespoon cornstarch**
**2 tablespoons water**

Prepare Mushroom Stuffing; set aside. Preheat oven to 350F (175C). Lightly rub chicken, inside and out, with salt. Fill chicken cavity with stuffing. Lightly sprinkle paprika and pepper over outside of stuffed chicken. Place stuffed chicken in a roasting pan. Cover and bake 1 hour. Uncover; bake 30 minutes or until juices run clear when a knife is inserted between breast and thigh. Place chicken on a platter. Prepare Gravy. Makes 4 servings.

**Mushroom Stuffing:**
Heat wine and 1 tablespoon butter or margarine in a large skillet. Add mushrooms; cook over medium-low heat until tender. Remove mushrooms from cooking juices; set aside. Add liver to cooking juices. Cook over medium-low heat until tender. Remove liver; set aside. Reserve cooking juices for gravy. Melt 2 tablespoons butter or margarine in a large skillet. Add stale bread or croutons; sauté over medium heat until bread begins to brown. Let cool. Stir sautéed mushrooms and liver, pepper, nutmeg, salt and parsley into stuffing bread. Add beaten eggs. Lightly mix with a fork to combine.

**Gravy:**
In a small saucepan, combine chicken-liver cooking juices, Maggi seasoning, wine and broth or bouillon. Blend cornstarch and water in a small bowl. Stir into gravy. Simmer over low heat, stirring constantly, 10 minutes or until thickened.

# Chicken Patties with Poached Eggs

Kotlety z Kury z Jajkami

*When turning these patties in the skillet, be careful so they don't break apart.*

1/4 cup milk
1 stale dinner roll
1 lb. cooked chicken, minced
1 egg
1/2 teaspoon salt
1/4 teaspoon freshly ground black pepper

1/2 teaspoon ground nutmeg
1 tablespoon chopped fresh parsley
3 tablespoons butter or margarine, melted
1/2 cup dry bread crumbs
Vegetable oil
6 eggs

Place milk in a large bowl. Break roll into pieces; soak roll pieces in milk. Mash soaked roll. Blend in chicken, egg, salt, pepper, nutmeg, parsley and butter or margarine. Shape chicken mixture into 6 (4- to 5-inch-round) patties. Place bread crumbs in a shallow dish. Carefully press both sides of each patty into crumbs until evenly coated. Heat 3 tablespoons oil in a large skillet. Add 3 patties; fry over medium heat 3 to 4 minutes on each side or until both sides are browned. Place browned patties on a plate; keep warm in oven. Brown remaining chicken patties, adding oil as needed. Poach 6 eggs in a large saucepan. To serve, carefully place 1 poached egg on each chicken patty. Makes 6 servings.

# Chicken Paprika

Paprykarz z Kury

*A simple, fast and zesty dish, usually served with rice.*

6 to 8 chicken-breast halves, skinned, boned
2 tablespoons butter or margarine
2 medium onions, sliced
1 teaspoon ground sweet paprika
Pinch of salt

Pinch of freshly ground black pepper
1-1/2 cups Chicken Broth, page 28,
   or bouillon
3 tablespoons dairy sour cream mixed with
   2 teaspoons all-purpose flour

Place chicken pieces between plastic wrap. Using a meat mallet, pound each piece to about 3/8 inch thick. Melt butter or margarine in a large skillet. Add 1/2 the chicken to skillet; sauté over medium heat 3 minutes per side. Remove breasts and set aside. Cook remaining chicken. Remove and add to other breasts. In skillet with chicken juices, place onions, paprika, salt and pepper. Sauté over medium heat, 10 minutes or until onions are tender. Add chicken. Add broth or bouillon. Cover and simmer 15 minutes. Remove breasts to a platter and keep warm. Stir in sour-cream mixture. Simmer, uncovered, 5 minutes or until liquid bubbles; do not boil. Makes 6 servings.

# Baked Cornish Hens

Mlode Kurczaki

*For best results, select firm, ripe tomatoes.*

1/4 cup butter or margarine
4 Cornish hens, thawed, if frozen,
   cut in halves
5 garlic cloves, crushed
1 tablespoon salt
1/4 teaspoon freshly ground black pepper

1/8 teaspoon ground thyme
1-1/2 cups dry white wine
4 medium tomatoes, peeled
1 tablespoon potato starch or cornstarch
   mixed with 1 tablespoon water

Preheat oven to 350F (175C). Melt butter or margarine in a large skillet. Add hen pieces; sauté over medium-low heat 10 minutes on each side or until both sides are golden brown. Arrange hen pieces in a shallow baking dish. Add cooking juices. Sprinkle hen pieces with garlic, salt, pepper and thyme. Cover and bake 20 to 25 minutes. Add wine to cooking juices. Slice tomatoes. Remove and discard tomato seeds. Arrange tomatoes over hen pieces. Cover; bake 15 minutes or until tender. Place hen pieces on a warm platter. Pour 1/4 cup cooking juices into a small saucepan. Stir in potato starch or cornstarch mixture until well blended. Pour in remaining cooking juices. Bring to a boil over medium heat, stirring constantly, until thickened. Reduce heat to low. Simmer 5 minutes. To serve, spoon sauce over hen pieces. Makes 4 servings.

# Cornish Hens Kaukas

Kurczaki po Kaukasku

*This spicy recipe originated in a mountainous region of Russia.*

6 garlic cloves, minced
About 2 teaspoons ground sweet paprika
2 tablespoons salt
1/2 teaspoon freshly ground black pepper

4 Cornish hens, thawed, if frozen
3 tablespoons vegetable oil
1 cup half and half
2 tablespoons lemon juice

In a small bowl, combine garlic, paprika, salt and pepper. Rub hens, inside and out, with garlic mixture. Heat oil in a large deep skillet. Brown hens evenly over medium heat. In a small bowl, combine half and half and lemon juice. Pour over hens. Place skillet over low heat. Cover with a tight-fitting lid. Simmer about 1 hour, turning hens once every 15 minutes. Serve hot. Makes 4 servings.

**Variation**

Preheat oven to 350F (175C). Place browned hens in a deep baking dish. Pour half and half mixture over hens. Bake, uncovered, 35 to 40 minutes or until tender.

# Goose Ragout

Pikantne Ragout z Gesi

*Try to find a grain-fed goose about five or six months old for this main dish.*

3 cups Chicken Broth, page 28, or bouillon
1 (8- to 9-lb.) goose, thaw, if frozen,
   then cut up
2 medium carrots, chopped
1 leek, chopped
1 parsley root, chopped
1 celery root, chopped
1-1/2 teaspoons salt
1/2 teaspoon freshly ground black pepper

1/4 teaspoon ground thyme
1/2 oz. dried mushrooms, chopped
2 tablespoons butter or margarine
2 medium onions, chopped
2 tablespoons tomato paste
1 tablespoon all-purpose flour
1/2 cup red wine
Cooked white rice

Heat broth or bouillon in a large saucepan. Add goose. Cover with a tight-fitting lid. Simmer over low heat 45 minutes, turning several times. Add carrots, leek, parsley root, celery root, salt, pepper, thyme and mushrooms. Cook, covered, over low heat 1 hour or until goose is tender. Remove goose from skillet; let cool 10 minutes. Reserve cooking liquid and vegetables. Remove goose meat from bones; discard bones. Cut cooked goose meat into bite-sized pieces. Melt butter or margarine in a large skillet. Add onions; sauté over medium-low heat until tender. Stir tomato paste, flour and wine into sautéed onions. Add goose meat, reserved cooked vegetables and cooking liquid. Bring to a boil over medium heat. Serve over hot rice. Makes 8 to 10 servings.

# Roast Duckling

Nadziewana Kaczka

*The sweet and sour Cumberland Sauce adds just the right touch to the distinctive roast-duckling flavor.*

1 (4-1/2- to 5-lb.) duck, thawed, if frozen
1 teaspoon salt
3 garlic cloves, minced

1/2 cup water
3 medium apples
Cumberland Sauce, page 67

Preheat oven to 350F (175C). Remove giblets and neck from duck cavity. Rinse duck under cold running water; pat dry with paper towels. Remove any excess fat from duck; discard fat. Prick duck skin all over to let fat drain during roasting. Rub duck, inside and out, with salt and garlic. Place duck, breast-side up, on a rack in a shallow roasting pan. Pour water in bottom of roasting pan. Place whole apples in duck cavity. Roast duck 1-1/2 to 2 hours or until juices run clear when a knife is inserted between breast and thigh. While duck is cooking, prepare Cumberland Sauce. Cool duck slightly. Using a heavy cleaver or knife, cut duck into quarters. Place duck quarters, skin-side up, in a shallow baking dish. Spoon Cumberland Sauce over duck. Preheat broiler. Broil 4 to 5 minutes or until sauce bubbles. Serve immediately with cooked apples. Makes 2 to 4 servings.

# Stuffed Turkey

Indyk Nadziewany

*The strong liver flavor dominates this old-fashioned Polish stuffed turkey.*

| | |
|---|---|
| 1 (8- to 10-lb.) turkey, thawed, if frozen | 2 cups dry bread crumbs |
| 1 tablespoon plus 1/2 teaspoon salt | 1/4 teaspoon freshly ground black pepper |
| 1/2 cup water | 1/4 teaspoon ground cloves |
| 3 eggs, separated | 1/4 teaspoon ground nutmeg |
| 2 tablespoons butter or margarine, room temperature | 1/4 cup raisins |
| 1 turkey liver, minced | 1/2 cup butter or margarine, melted |
| 1-1/2 tablespoons chopped fresh parsley | Red wine, if desired |

Preheat oven to 325F (165C). Remove giblets and neck from turkey cavity; reserve for stock or soup. Rinse turkey under cold running water; blot dry. Rub turkey, inside and out, with 1 tablespoon salt. Place turkey, breast-side down, on a rack in a shallow roasting pan. Pour water into roasting pan. In a medium bowl, beat egg yolks and 2 tablespoons butter or margarine until pale and creamy. Add liver, parsley, bread crumbs, 1/2 teaspoon salt, pepper, cloves, nutmeg and raisins. In a medium bowl, beat egg whites until stiff peaks form; fold into egg-yolk mixture. Spoon resulting mixture into turkey cavity. Roast 3-1/2 to 4 hours or until juices run clear when a knife is inserted between breast and thigh. Baste with butter or margarine every 20 minutes. Place turkey on a large platter. Cover with foil and let stand 20 to 30 minutes before carving. Serve with stuffing. Pour pan juices into a small saucepan, if desired. Place over medium heat. Add red wine, if desired. Cook, stirring constantly, 3 to 4 minutes. Spoon cooked juices over turkey slices and stuffing. Makes 12 to 14 servings.

# Normandy Turkey   Photo on pages 2 & 3.

Indyk po Normandzku

*Combining butter-basted turkey and aromatic Polish white sausage creates a special dinner.*

| | |
|---|---|
| 1 (8- to 8-1/2-lb.) turkey, thawed, if frozen | 1/2 cup butter or margarine, melted |
| 1 tablespoon salt | 2 tablespoons cognac |
| 1/2 teaspoon freshly ground black pepper | 1 cup Chicken Broth, page 28, or bouillon |
| 10 small apples, peeled | 1-1/2 lbs. Polish white sausage or fresh Polish sausage |

Preheat oven to 350F (175C). Remove giblets and neck from turkey cavity; reserve for stock or soup. Rinse turkey under cold running water; blot dry. Rub turkey, inside and out, with salt and pepper. Place turkey on a rack, breast-side down, in a shallow roasting pan. Arrange peeled apples in turkey cavity. In a small bowl, combine butter or margarine and cognac. Pour broth or bouillon into roasting pan. Roast turkey 2 hours, basting every 15 minutes with cognac mixture. Twist sausage into small links. Prick each link with a fork to let juices escape during cooking. After 2 hours cooking, place sausage links around turkey on bottom of roasting pan. Roast turkey and sausage 30 minutes to 1 hour or until juices run clear when a knife is inserted between breast and thigh. Place turkey on a large platter. Keep sausage warm in oven. Cover turkey with foil and let stand 20 to 30 minutes before carving. Before carving, arrange warm sausage links around turkey on platter. Makes 8 to 10 servings.

# Spinach Omelet

Omlet ze Szpinakiem

*The sweet red-pepper sauce gives this omelet a special taste dimension.*

2 tablespoons and 1 teaspoon butter or
  margarine
1 garlic clove, minced
1/2 pickled sweet red pepper or pimento,
  sliced
1 tablespoon chopped fresh parsley
1 small tomato, chopped

1/2 teaspoon olive oil
1/2 cup chopped fresh spinach
2 eggs
1 tablespoon cold water
1/2 teaspoon salt
1/8 teaspoon ground white pepper

Melt 1 tablespoon butter or margarine in a small skillet. Add garlic, red pepper or pimento, parsley and tomato. Sauté over medium-low heat 3 to 4 minutes. Remove from heat; keep warm in
oven. Heat oil and 1 teaspoon butter or margarine in a small skillet. Add spinach. Sauté over low
heat, 4 to 5 minutes. Melt 1 tablespoon butter or margarine in a medium skillet. In a medium
bowl, beat eggs, water, salt and white pepper. Pour egg mixture into skillet. Cook over medium-
low heat. Using a spatula, lift edges of eggs when they set. When eggs are half set, sprinkle sautéed
spinach over 1/2 of omelet. Cook until eggs are almost set, freeing omelet from skillet bottom
with spatula. Carefully fold omelet in 1/2 with spatula. Cook 1 minute. Turn omelet over; cook 1
minute. Serve immediately with red-pepper mixture over omelet. Makes 1 serving.

# Omelet with Peas

Omlet z Groszkiem

*Surprise your guests with this delicious and unusual dish.*

Dill Sauce with Sour Cream, page 56,
  if desired
1 cup fresh or frozen green peas
1/4 cup plus 1 teaspoon butter or margarine
1 small onion, chopped

8 eggs
3 tablespoons half and half or milk
1 teaspoon salt
1/4 teaspoon freshly ground black pepper

Prepare Dill Sauce with Sour Cream, if desired. Place peas and 1 tablespoon butter or margarine
in a small saucepan. Add enough salted water to cover. Bring to a boil over medium-high heat.
Reduce heat to low. Cover and simmer 5 to 7 minutes or until tender. Drain. Melt 1 teaspoon
butter or margarine in a small skillet. Add onion; sauté over medium heat until tender. Stir
cooked onion into peas. Place eggs, half and half or milk, salt and pepper in a medium bowl. Beat
lightly with a fork until combined. Melt remaining 3 tablespoons butter or margarine in a large
skillet. Pour egg mixture into skillet. Cook over medium heat. Using a spatula, lift edges of eggs
when they set. When eggs are half set, sprinkle peas and onion over 1/2 of omelet. Cook until
eggs are almost set, freeing omelet from skillet bottom with spatula. Carefully fold omelet in 1/2
with spatula. Cook 1 minute. Turn omelet over; cook 1 minute. Serve immediately with warm
Dill Sauce with Sour Cream, if desired. Makes 4 servings.

# Bull's-Eye Eggs

Wolowe Oczy Jajka

*A creative way to use common ingredients in a tasty and attractive dish.*

**4 slices white bread**
**Butter or margarine, room temperature**
**4 eggs**
**2 tablespoons half and half**
**Salt**

**Freshly ground black pepper**
**1/3 cup shredded sharp Cheddar cheese**
  **(1-1/2 oz.)**
**Finely chopped parsley**

Preheat oven to 325F (165C). Cut out a 2-1/2-inch circle from center of each bread slice, leaving crust intact. Discard bread circles or reserve for another use. Lightly spread butter or margarine on 1 side of each bread piece. Heat a large skillet. Add bread, buttered side down. Cook over medium heat until lightly browned. Turn bread over; cook 1 minute. Remove from skillet. Lightly grease a large shallow baking dish. Place each bread piece in baking dish. Break 1 egg into each bread crust. Drizzle 1-1/2 teaspoons half and half over each egg. Season with salt and pepper to taste. Top bread crusts with shredded cheese. Bake 15 to 20 minutes or until egg whites set. Garnish with parsley. Makes 4 servings.

# Farmer's Eggs

Jajecznica Gospodarska

*Some brave farmers use two or three times the amount of recommended pepper.*

**1/2 lb. bacon slices**
**2 medium tomatoes, peeled**
**1-1/2 tablespoons butter or margarine**
**2 garlic cloves, crushed**

**1/2 teaspoon salt**
**1/4 teaspoon freshly ground black pepper**
**6 eggs, beaten**
**2 tablespoons chopped chives**

Cut each bacon slice into thirds. In a small skillet, fry bacon over medium heat until crisp. Drain on paper towels. Cut each tomato into 8 wedges. Cut wedges in 1/2. Melt butter or margarine in a medium skillet. Add tomatoes, garlic, salt and pepper. Sauté over medium heat, stirring gently until tomatoes are cooked but not too soft, about 2 to 3 minutes. Add cooked bacon; sauté 1 minute. Add eggs; gently stir over medium-low heat until cooked as desired. Place in a serving dish. Garnish with chives. Makes 4 servings.

# Shirred Eggs

Pieczone Jajka

*Cooked to perfection, these baked eggs have soft yolks and lightly set whites.*

**2 tablespoons half and half**
**2 tablespoons minced ham**
**2 eggs**

**Salt**
**Freshly ground black pepper**
**Pinch of chopped fresh parsley**

Preheat oven to 325F (165C). Rub a ramekin or small round baking dish with butter, margarine or olive oil. Place half and half and ham in greased dish. Break eggs into dish. Sprinkle with salt and pepper. Garnish with parsley. Bake 15 to 20 minutes or until egg whites are set. Serve immediately. Makes 1 serving.

# How to Make Bull's-Eye Eggs

1/Place each toasted bread piece in greased shallow baking dish. Break 1 egg into each bread crust.

2/Top bread crusts with shredded cheese. Bake 15 to 20 minutes or until egg whites set. Garnish with parsley.

# Egg Cutlets

Kotlety z Jaj

*In Poland, this dish is prepared as a flavorful substitute for meat.*

**Mushroom Sauce, page 69**
**4 hard-cooked eggs**
**1 large stale hard roll**
**1/2 cup milk**
**2 tablespoons chopped fresh chives**
**1/4 cup butter or margarine,**
**    room temperature**

**1 egg**
**3/4 teaspoon salt**
**1/4 teaspoon freshly ground black pepper**
**About 1/2 cup dry bread crumbs**

Prepare Mushroom Sauce. Using a grinder, grind hard-cooked eggs or finely chop. Cut roll in 1/2; soak both halves in a small bowl with milk. Squeeze excess milk from roll. Discard milk. In a medium bowl, combine chives and 1 tablespoon butter or margarine. Add ground eggs, raw egg, salt, pepper and soaked roll. On a flat working surface, spread out 1/4 cup dry bread crumbs evenly over an area about 8" x 5". Place egg mixture on center of bread crumbs. Carefully shape a loaf about 10" by 3" inches and 1-1/2" inches high. Press bread crumbs evenly into the surface. Let stand at room temperature 5 minutes. With a sharp knife, cut crosswise into 1-inch slices. Cover both sides of slices with remaining 1/4 cup bread crumbs. Melt 3 tablespoons butter or margarine in a large skillet. Add egg cutlets; cook over medium heat about 1-1/2 to 2 minutes on each side or until both sides are browned. Serve hot with Mushroom Sauce. Makes 10 cutlets.

# PORK &

Imagine going back centuries in Poland, to a place where a band of disheveled hunters gather around a simmering pot full of aromatic ingredients. If you could listen to the hunters, you'd hear them tell exciting, animated stories of the chase, while they patiently wait long into the night for the pot's contents to cook to perfection.

Nine out of ten times, they were preparing Bigos. Bigos, or *Hunter's Stew,* is the most traditional of all Polish dishes. Even today, it is still prepared after deer, bear and wild boar hunts, using meat from the quarry. This is combined with pork, beef, kielbasa, sauerkraut and other ingredients that blend in true harmony.

Bigos is included in this chapter because pork is still the main meat ingredient. Bigos is a dish that improves with age. In fact, it was common for hunters to simmer Bigos for several days, while celebrating the end of a hunting season or other major event.

Bigos is only one of the many ways pork is featured in Polish cuisine. More people in Poland raise hogs or pigs than steers. A typical village family might keep three or four hogs per year, feeding them grain, vegetables or table scraps. And hogs don't need large fields to graze in. Because pork is more readily available than beef, it finds its way into a larger variety of dishes.

Another special recipe is Vienna Pork Rolls, in which thick slices of pork loin are tenderized and salted. Then they're rolled up with a delightful filling of sautéed chopped ham and sour cream seasoned with thyme and garlic.

The most common pork dish is the simple, no-frill cutlet—tenderized boneless loin slices, breaded and sautéed until golden, sometimes with a surprising addition of a thin slice of Gouda, mozzarella or provolone cheese.

From cutlets on, the pork pieces get smaller. In Bialystok Pork, they're slender strips sautéed with sliced mushrooms, onion and green pepper,

## Bialystok Pork

Przysmak Bialostocki

*This recipe is a favorite of all three of my brothers.*

2 tablespoons butter or margarine
1 lb. fresh mushrooms, sliced
2 lbs. lean boneless pork
2 tablespoons vegetable oil
1 medium onion, chopped

1 small green bell pepper, chopped
2 tablespoons Maggi seasoning
1 teaspoon ground ginger
Cooked rice, if desired

Melt butter or margarine in a large skillet. Add mushrooms; sauté over medium heat until tender. Remove from heat. Slice pork in 1/2-inch-thick strips, about 3-1/2 inches long. Heat oil in a large skillet. Add pork strips; sauté over medium heat until evenly browned. Remove pork from skillet. Place onion and green pepper in pork drippings; sauté until tender. Return pork to skillet. Add sautéed mushrooms, Maggi seasoning and ginger. Cook, uncovered, over low heat 20 minutes or until cooked through, stirring occasionally. Serve over cooked rice, if desired. Makes 4 to 6 servings.

# LAMB

seasoned with the Polish substitute for soy sauce—Maggi Seasoning—and sprinkled with ground ginger.

Another traditional way to prepare pork is to smoke it. Smoked pork loin is usually eaten cold, sliced for the appetizer tray, or used as a filling for sandwiches.

When my husband and I were married in Poland, the morning after our farmhouse reception, he helped my father return borrowed tables and chairs to our neighbors. After hauling a particularly heavy wood table into the thatched-roof home of its owner—a wrinkled, toothless bachelor in his 70s, my husband was offered what he thought was a square piece of cheese, along with a shot of Polish spiritus or vodka.

My husband popped the "cheese" into his mouth, only to discover that in truth, it was a chunk of bacon fat. For one time, the spiritus came in handy. Among the older generation in Poland, plain smoked bacon fat is considered a delicacy.

Lamb is not as important to the Polish diet as it was years ago, when sheep were often raised for their wool. Yet the taste for lamb lingers on in many of the older segments of the population.

Lamb is a tender meat with a distinctive flavor all its own. The meat itself is covered with a thin membrane that feels like paper and is called the *fell*. The fell is generally removed before cooking.

An old standby, Lamb Cutlet, is flavored with ground sweet paprika and garlic, then simmered until tender in cooking juices of broth, butter or margarine and onions.

Roast Lamb is begun by wrapping a boneless lamb roast with vinegar-soaked cheesecloth, then refrigerating the roast. A later step finds slivers of garlic inserted in narrow slits cut throughout the roast's surface before the meat is browned and cooked.

# Stuffed Cabbage   Photo on cover.

Golabki

*Worldwide, this is one of the most popular and best-known Polish dishes.*

| | |
|---|---|
| 1 (3-lb.) head green cabbage | 1 teaspoon salt |
| 1/4 cup butter or margarine | 1/4 teaspoon freshly ground black pepper |
| 1 small onion, chopped | 3-1/2 cups Beef Broth, page 27, or bouillon |
| 1 lb. lean ground beef | 1 (6-oz.) can tomato paste |
| 1-1/2 lbs. lean ground pork | 2 tablespoons all-purpose flour |
| 1-1/2 cups cooked long-grain white rice | |

With a sharp knife, remove core from cabbage. Carefully remove wilted or decayed outer cabbage leaves; discard. In a large saucepan, boil enough salted water to cover cabbage. Immerse cabbage in boiling water. Cook over medium-high heat 5 to 7 minutes. With fork or tongs, gently remove leaves as they become tender. Drain well; let cool. Preheat oven to 325F (165C). Trim main leaf stems. Melt 1 tablespoon butter or margarine in a small skillet. Add onion; sauté over medium heat until golden brown. In a large bowl, combine sautéed onion, beef, pork, rice, salt and pepper. Spread a cabbage leaf flat. Depending on leaf size, place 2 to 3 tablespoons filling on cabbage leaf near base. Fold bottom of leaf over filling, then fold sides toward center. Roll tightly. Repeat with remaining filling and cabbage leaves. Heat 1 tablespoon butter or margarine in a large skillet. Place filled cabbage leaves, seam down, in skillet. Cook over medium heat until browned, 8 to 10 minutes, turning once with a spatula. Arrange cabbage rolls, seam-side down, in a medium roasting pan. Add 3 cups broth or bouillon. In a small bowl, combine 1/2 cup broth or bouillon and tomato paste. Pour over stuffed cabbage. Cover and bake 40 minutes or until fork-tender. In a small skillet, melt remaining 2 tablespoons butter or margarine. Stir flour into butter or margarine until smooth. Cook over medium heat, stirring, until golden brown. Ladle 1 cup broth or bouillon from stuffed cabbage into flour mixture; blend. Pour mixture over stuffed cabbage. Cook, uncovered, until liquid bubbles and thickens slightly. Place stuffed cabbage on a large platter. Pour pan juices into a serving bowl. Serve hot with pan juices. Makes 10 to 12 servings.

# How to Make Stuffed Cabbage

1/With fork or tongs, gently remove outer cabbage leaves as they become tender. Drain well.

2/Using a paring knife, trim heavy leaf stems for ease in rolling stuffed cabbage.

3/Place 2 to 3 tablespoons filling on cabbage leaf near base. Fold bottom of leaf over filling.

4/Then fold sides toward center. Roll tightly, enclosing filling completely.

# Baked Pork Loin

Pieczona Poledwica Wieprzowa

*In Poland, apples and pork often find their way into the same dishes.*

| | |
|---|---|
| **1 teaspoon salt** | **3 tablespoons vegetable oil** |
| **1 teaspoon freshly ground black pepper** | **2 medium onions, chopped** |
| **1/4 teaspoon ground marjoram** | **3 medium, tart apples, peeled, shredded** |
| **1 (4-lb.) bone-in pork-loin roast** | **1 cup water** |
| **All-purpose flour** | |

Combine salt, pepper and marjoram in a small bowl. Pat roast dry. Rub roast with salt mixture. Let stand 15 minutes. Sprinkle roast with flour until evenly coated. Preheat oven to 325F (165C). Heat oil in a large skillet. Add roast; cook over medium-high heat until browned on all sides. Place browned roast in a deep baking dish. Add onions to skillet cooking juices; sauté over medium heat until tender. Remove from heat. Stir apples into onions; spoon mixture over roast. Add water to bottom of baking dish. Cook, uncovered, 2 to 2-1/2 hours or until tender. Baste every 20 minutes, adding enough water to make sure at least 1 cup cooking juices remains in baking dish throughout cooking time. When done, remove meat and strain cooking juices. Slice meat and serve hot with side dish of strained juices. Makes 6 to 8 servings.

# Boneless Pork Loin    Photo on pages 2 & 3.

Schab Pieczony

*In Poland, this cut of meat is usually saved for the holidays.*

| | |
|---|---|
| **1 (3-lb.) boneless pork-loin roast** | **1/2 teaspoon freshly ground black pepper** |
| **5 garlic cloves, crushed** | **3 medium onions, thinly sliced** |
| **1 tablespoon salt** | **1/2 cup Meat Broth, page 27, or bouillon** |
| **2 tablespoons vegetable oil** | |

Pat pork roast dry. Combine garlic and salt in a small bowl. Rub roast with garlic mixture. Let stand 15 minutes. Heat oil in a large, deep skillet. Add roast; cook over medium-high heat until browned on all sides. Reduce heat to low. Sprinkle pepper over roast. Arrange onion slices on top of roast. Gently sprinkle broth over onions. Cover and simmer 2-1/2 hours or until tender, basting with cooking juices every 15 minutes, adding water if needed. To serve, slice and spoon cooked onions and juices over meat. Makes 6 servings.

## Variation

Substitute 1/2 teaspoon ground marjoram for pepper and 1 lb. peeled, sliced tart apples for onions. Serve as above.

# Wild-Pork Roast

Dzika Pieczen Wieprzowa

*This recipe was developed in the 17th century using wild boar.*

| | |
|---|---|
| 1-1/2 cups white wine | 3 medium onions |
| Juice of 1 lemon | Salt |
| 10 black peppercorns | 2 tablespoons vegetable oil |
| 2 whole cloves | 1 cup Chicken Broth, page 28, or bouillon |
| 1 bay leaf | 1 tablespoon jam, such as currant, |
| 1/4 teaspoon ground marjoram | cherry or raspberry |
| 1 (3-lb.) boneless pork-loin roast | 1 tablespoon all-purpose flour |

In a medium saucepan, combine wine, lemon juice, peppercorns, cloves, bay leaf and marjoram. Bring to boil over medium heat. Place pork loin in a deep, narrow non-metallic baking dish. Slice 2 of the onions and arrange slices over pork. Pour wine marinade over meat and onions. Cover with plastic wrap or foil. Refrigerate 2 to 3 days, turning meat twice per day. Preheat oven to 325F (165C). Remove meat from marinade; reserve marinade. Pat meat dry. Rub with salt. Heat oil in a medium skillet. Cook pork over medium-high heat until brown on all sides. Place pork in a deep, narrow baking dish. Bake, covered with a tight-fitting lid, 30 minutes. Slice remaining onion and arrange slices over pork. Bake, covered, 2 hours. Strain marinade into a medium bowl. In a small bowl, combine broth or bouillon, jam and flour. Stir into marinade. Pour resulting sauce over pork. Bake, uncovered, 20 to 30 minutes or until tender. Serve hot. Slice meat; ladle sauce over each portion. Makes 6 servings.

# Vienna Pork Rolls

Wiedenskie Sznycle

*Here's a unique way to prepare pork chops.*

| | |
|---|---|
| 4 (1-1/2-inch-thick) boneless | 1/4 teaspoon ground thyme |
| pork-loin slices | 2 garlic cloves, crushed |
| 1/2 teaspoon salt | 1 egg yolk |
| 3 tablespoons butter or margarine | 1 large onion, sliced |
| 1 cup chopped cooked ham | 1 cup Meat Broth, page 27, or bouillon |
| 6 tablespoons dairy sour cream | 1 tablespoon all-purpose flour |

Place pork slices between plastic wrap. Using a meat mallet, pound pork slices to ovals approximately 1/2 inch thick. Rub both sides of pork pieces with salt. Melt 1 tablespoon butter or margarine in a medium skillet. Add chopped ham; sauté over medium heat, stirring until browned. Reduce heat to low. Stir 3 tablespoons sour cream, thyme and garlic into sautéed meat. Simmer 10 minutes; do not boil. Let cool. Blend in egg yolk. Arrange pork pieces on a flat surface. Place 1/4 filling mixture on each pork piece. Roll up jelly-roll style; tie with string. Melt 2 tablespoons butter or margarine in a large skillet. Add onion; sauté over medium heat until tender. Remove onion from skillet; set aside. Place filled pork rolls in onion cooking juices. Sauté over medium heat until browned on all sides. Return sautéed onion to skillet. Add broth or bouillon. Cover with a tight-fitting lid; simmer over low heat 1 hour or until tender, turning occasionally. Remove pork rolls from skillet; keep warm. In a small bowl, blend remaining 3 tablespoons sour cream and flour. Gently stir into cooking juices. Simmer 10 minutes or until slightly thickened; do not boil. Serve rolls hot with sauce. Makes 4 servings.

# How to Make Pork & Cheese Cutlets

1/Place 1 cheese slice on each pork piece; pat cheese firmly onto meat. Dip meat in flour, being careful to cover both sides.

2/Dip each floured pork piece in egg, then in bread crumbs. Press bread crumbs evenly onto meat.

# Pork & Cheese Cutlets

Kotlety Schabowe z Serem

*The cheese in this recipe will pleasantly surprise your dinner guests.*

**2 lbs. boneless pork loin, cut in
    10 to 12 (1/2-inch-thick) slices
Salt
Freshly ground black pepper
10 to 12 (3-inch-square) thin slices Gouda,
    mozzarella or provolone cheese**

**1/2 cup all-purpose flour
2 eggs, beaten
1/2 cup dry bread crumbs
2 tablespoons butter or margarine**

Place pork pieces between 2 pieces of plastic wrap. Using a meat mallet, pound each side until pork pieces are about 1/4 to 3/8 inch thick. Season pork pieces with salt and pepper. Preheat oven to 350F (175C). Place 1 cheese slice on each piece of meat. Pat cheese firmly onto meat. Place flour, eggs and bread crumbs in separate shallow dishes. Dip meat in flour, being careful to cover both sides, including cheese. Shake off excess. Dip each piece in egg, then in bread crumbs. Press bread crumbs evenly onto meat. Melt butter or margarine in a large skillet. Add meat, cheese-side up; cook over medium heat, 7 to 10 minutes or until browned on both sides. Grease a large baking dish. Arrange meat, cheese-side up, in dish so pieces do not touch each other. Bake, uncovered, 20 minutes or until tender. Makes 6 servings.

# Pork Cutlets

Kotlety Schabowe

*A simple-to-make, tasty, no-waste main dish.*

| | |
|---|---|
| 6 thick pork-loin rib chops | 1/2 teaspoon ground sweet paprika |
| 3/4 cup all-purpose flour | 2 eggs, beaten |
| 1 teaspoon salt | 1 cup dry bread crumbs |
| 1/2 teaspoon freshly ground black pepper | 1/3 cup vegetable oil |

Bone pork chops. Trim excess fat from meat. Score 1-inch cuts at 3 places on each pork-chop edge to prevent curling while cooking. Place pork pieces between 2 pieces of plastic wrap. Using a meat mallet, pound 5 times on each side or until pork pieces are about 1/2 inch thick. Combine flour, salt, pepper and paprika in a shallow dish. Place eggs and bread crumbs in separate shallow dishes. Dip pounded pork pieces in flour mixture, then dip in egg and bread crumbs, pressing bread crumbs evenly onto pork. Place breaded pork pieces on a rack. Let stand 15 minutes. Heat oil in a large skillet. Add pork cutlets. Cook over medium-low heat, turning occasionally, 20 minutes or until cooked through. Makes 6 servings.

# Hash Polish Style

Zapiekanka

*The combination of sour cream and mushrooms contrasts nicely with pork and potato flavors.*

| | |
|---|---|
| 1/2 oz. dried mushrooms | 2 medium onions, chopped |
| 2-1/2 cups water | 1/8 teaspoon freshly ground black pepper |
| 3 lbs. baking potatoes, peeled, sliced | 1 teaspoon chopped fresh parsley |
| 1 teaspoon salt | 1/2 pint dairy sour cream (1 cup) |
| 2 tablespoons butter or margarine | 1 tablespoon all-purpose flour |
| 1 lb. pork strips | |
|   (1/4 inch thick, 1 inch long) | |

Wash mushrooms; place in a small saucepan. Add 2-1/2 cups water. Cover; simmer over low heat until rehydrated, about 25 to 30 minutes. Drain; reserve liquid. Let mushrooms cool. Place potatoes and salt in a large saucepan; cover with water. Bring to a boil; cook until tender. Drain potatoes; set aside. Melt butter or margarine in a large skillet. Add pork strips and onions; sauté over medium-low heat until pork browns and onions are tender, about 30 minutes. Add 2/3 cup reserved mushroom liquid. Reduce heat to low. Simmer, uncovered, 5 minutes. Chop cooked mushrooms. Stir mushrooms, pepper and parsley into pork mixture. Simmer 5 minutes. Preheat oven to 350F (175C). Grease a 9-inch-square baking dish. Arrange 1/3 of potatoes evenly on bottom of greased dish. Cover with 1/2 of pork mixture; pat into an even layer. In a small bowl, combine sour cream, flour and remaining mushroom liquid. Pour 1/3 of sour-cream mixture over pork layer. Add another 1/3 of potatoes in a layer and remaining pork in a layer. Spread with 1/2 of remaining sour-cream mixture. Layer remaining potatoes over sour-cream mixture. Spread with remaining sour-cream mixture. Smooth surface with a spoon. Bake, uncovered, 40 minutes or until top layer of sour cream sets and turns a dull, pale brown. Makes 8 servings.

# Spareribs Polish Style

Zeberka po Polsku

*For preparation ease, have your butcher cut the ribs into serving-size pieces.*

1/4 cup all-purpose flour
2 lbs. pork spareribs, cut in pieces
2 tablespoons vegetable oil
4 medium onions, sliced
1 (6-oz.) can tomato paste

2 cups Beef Broth, page 27;
    Chicken Broth, page 28; or bouillon
1 teaspoon salt
1/2 teaspoon freshly ground black pepper

Place flour in a shallow dish. Roll spareribs in flour until evenly coated. Heat oil in a large skillet. Add floured ribs; cook over medium heat 20 to 30 minutes until evenly browned. Remove browned ribs from skillet. Place on a plate; set aside. Add onions to skillet; sauté until tender. Return ribs to skillet. In a small bowl, combine tomato paste and broth or bouillon. Gently stir tomato mixture into rib mixture. Season with salt and pepper. Cover and simmer 40 minutes or until tender. Makes 4 servings.

### Variation

Preheat oven to 350F (175C). Prepare recipe as above through sautéing onions. Place browned spareribs in a shallow baking dish. Top with sautéed onions, tomato-paste mixture and seasonings. Cover and bake 45 minutes or until tender.

# Beer Sausage

Kielbasa w Piwnym Sosie

*Polish sausage fixed a delightfully Polish way.*

3 lbs. Polish sausage
1 (12-oz.) can or bottle light beer
1-1/2 cups water
2 large onions, chopped
1 tablespoon butter or margarine
1 tablespoon all-purpose flour

Juice from 1 lemon
1 teaspoon sugar
1/2 teaspoon salt
1 teaspoon Maggi seasoning
Chopped fresh parsley

Place sausage in a large saucepan. Add beer, water and onions. Cover and cook over medium-high heat 20 minutes. Remove sausage; place in a casserole. Keep warm in oven. Strain sausage stock into a medium saucepan. Press onions through a strainer with a wooden spoon. Melt butter or margarine in a small skillet. Add flour, stirring until well blended. Stir over low heat 2 to 3 minutes or until mixture turns a golden color. Remove from heat. Stir in 2 tablespoons strained stock. Add lemon juice, sugar, salt and Maggi seasoning. Bring to a boil, stirring constantly. Combine with stock. Bring resulting sauce to a boil over medium heat. Pour thickened sauce over sausage. Garnish with parsley. Makes 6 servings.

# Pork & Vegetable Goulash

Gulasz Wieprzowy z Jarzynami

*Instead of all pork, substitute half veal or beef.*

1/2 cup all-purpose flour
1 teaspoon salt
1/8 teaspoon freshly ground black pepper
1-1/2 lbs. lean pork, cut into 1-inch cubes
1 tablespoon butter or margarine
3-1/2 cups Meat Broth, page 27, or bouillon
1 medium onion, chopped

1/2 cup shredded carrot
1/4 cup shredded parsley root
1/2 cup chopped leek
1/2 cup chopped celery
3 medium tomatoes, peeled, quartered
Cooked rice or noodles

In a plastic bag, combine flour, salt and pepper. Add pork cubes; shake until well coated. Melt butter or margarine in a large skillet. Sauté seasoned pork pieces in butter or margarine over medium-high heat 8 to 10 minutes or until evenly browned. Add broth or bouillon. Cover and simmer 20 minutes. Add onion, carrot, parsley root, leek and celery. Cover; simmer 30 minutes or until vegetables are tender. Add tomatoes. Cover; simmer 5 to 10 minutes or until tomatoes are cooked. Serve hot over cooked rice or noodles. Makes 6 servings.

# Pork Patties

Kotlety Mielone

*Serve these economical patties with Dill Sauce with Sour Cream, page 56, or Mushroom Sauce, page 69.*

1/4 cup milk
1 large stale hard roll
1-1/2 lbs. lean ground pork
1 egg
3 tablespoons chopped fresh dill or
   1 tablespoon dill weed

1 teaspoon salt
1/4 teaspoon freshly ground black pepper
1/3 cup dry bread crumbs
1/4 cup vegetable oil
1/2 cup Meat Broth, page 27, or bouillon

Place milk in a medium bowl. Break roll apart; add to milk. Soak until milk is absorbed. Blend in pork, egg, dill, salt and pepper. On a flat surface, shape into 6 (1-inch-thick) patties. Place bread crumbs in a shallow dish. Dip pork patties in bread crumbs, lightly pressing bread crumbs evenly onto pork. Heat oil in a large skillet. Add breaded pork patties; sauté over medium heat 10 to 12 minutes, until both sides are browned. Add broth or bouillon to skillet. Reduce heat to low. Simmer, uncovered, 10 minutes, turning once. Serve hot. Makes 6 servings.

# Scrambled Eggs & Smoked Pork Loin

Jajecznica z Wedzona Poledwica

*Probably the most popular scrambled-egg recipe, usually served with fresh hard rolls and butter.*

**12 (1/4-inch-thick) slices smoked pork loin**     **8 eggs**
**1 tablespoon butter or margarine**

Cut pork into 1/2- to 1-inch pieces. Melt butter or margarine in a large skillet. Add pork; sauté over medium-low heat until lightly browned on both sides. Break eggs into a medium bowl; beat lightly. With a fork, gently stir eggs into pork. Stir constantly so eggs will not stick. When eggs set but are still moist, remove from heat. Serve immediately. Makes 4 servings.

### Variations

Add 1/4 cup chopped onion when sautéing pork.

Substitute 4 cups sliced Polish sausage, cooked and drained, or 4 cups sliced fresh mushrooms for smoked pork loin.

# Hunter's Stew

Bigos

*A harmonious blend of flavors known as the Polish national dish.*

**3 lbs. sauerkraut**
**2 lbs. ham with bone, pork spareribs or**
    **pork rib roast**
**2 bay leaves**
**1 oz. dried mushrooms, chopped**
**20 black peppercorns**
**10 allspice berries**
**1/2 teaspoon salt**
**11 cups Beef Broth, page 27,**
    **bouillon or water**

**2 lbs. green cabbage,**
    **chopped like sauerkraut**
**2 tablespoons butter or margarine**
**1 lb. Polish smoked sausage,**
    **cut into 1/2-inch cubes**
**1 lb. Polish white sausage with garlic,**
    **cut into 1/2-inch cubes**
**1 lb. bacon, cut into 1/2-inch cubes**

Rinse sauerkraut with cold water; drain well. In a large stockpot, combine sauerkraut, ham or pork, bay leaves, mushrooms, peppercorns, allspice and salt. Add 6 cups broth, bouillon or water. Cook, uncovered, 15 minutes over medium heat. Cover and simmer over low heat 45 minutes. Remove meat. Let meat cool. Place cabbage in a large saucepan. Add remaining 5 cups broth, bouillon or water. Bring to boil. Cook, uncovered, over medium heat, 1 hour or until cabbage is tender. Add to sauerkraut mixture. Bone cooked meat. Cut cooked meat into 1/2-inch cubes. Melt butter or margarine in a large skillet. Add cooked meat, smoked sausage and white sausage. Sauté over medium heat 10 minutes or until browned. Add to sauerkraut mixture. In same skillet, sauté bacon over medium heat until crisp. Drain bacon on paper towels. Add to sauerkraut mixture. Cover; cook over low heat 1 hour or longer. Remove and discard bay leaves. Serve hot. Makes 12 to 14 servings.

*Use only meat with large bones, so bones can be removed easily. The secret of old-time Bigos is that it gets better as it's reheated on successive days, peaking at the 6th or 7th day. In between, store covered in the refrigerator.*

Hunter's Stew

# How to Make Roast Lamb

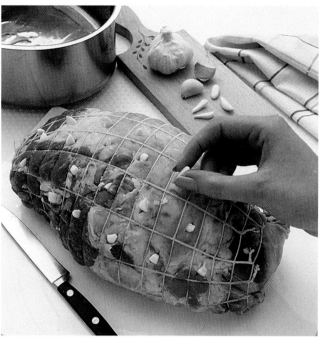

1/Wrap lamb tightly with vinegar-soaked cheesecloth. Cover and refrigerate up to 2 days.

2/Using a sharp knife, cut small deep slits evenly spaced over roast. Insert garlic slivers in slits.

## Roast Lamb

Pieczen Barania

*Cheesecloth soaked in white vinegar provides a custom marinade for this choice cut of lamb.*

**1 (5-1/2- to 6-lb.) boneless lamb roast**
**1/2 cup white vinegar**
**Salt**

**8 garlic cloves, slivered**
**1/4 cup all-purpose flour**
**1/2 to 1 cup water**

Place lamb in a shallow baking dish. In a bowl, soak a large piece of cheesecloth in vinegar. Remove cheesecloth from bowl; do not squeeze out. Wrap lamb tightly with cheesecloth. Cover; refrigerate up to 2 days. Rinse lamb with cold water. Pat dry. Preheat oven to 350F (175C). Lightly oil a small roasting pan. Sprinkle roast with salt. Using a sharp knife, cut small deep slits evenly spaced over roast. Insert garlic slivers in slits. Evenly sprinkle roast with flour. Place roast in oiled pan. Cook over medium heat until evenly browned. Add water to pan. Roast, uncovered, 3 hours or until tender. Baste with cooking juices every 20 minutes, adding water as necessary. Makes 14 to 16 servings.

# Lamb Cutlets

Kotlety Baranie

*The Pole's fondness for sweet paprika is reflected in yet another distinctive main dish.*

| | |
|---|---|
| 2-1/2 to 3 lbs. boneless lamb,<br>   cut in 1-inch-thick pieces | 2 tablespoons butter or margarine |
| 1 tablespoon ground sweet paprika | 8 garlic cloves, crushed |
| 1-1/2 teaspoons salt | 2 medium onions, chopped |
| 1 tablespoon all-purpose flour | 3 cups Chicken Broth, page 28, or bouillon |
| 2 tablespoons vegetable oil | 2 tablespoons cornstarch |
| | 1/4 cup water |

Place lamb pieces between plastic wrap. Using a meat mallet, pound lamb until 1/2 inch thick. Combine paprika, salt and flour in a small bowl. Dip lamb pieces in paprika mixture. Let stand 20 minutes. Heat oil in a large, heavy skillet. Add lamb; sauté over medium heat until evenly browned. Melt butter or margarine in a medium skillet. Add garlic and onions; sauté over medium heat until tender. Add sautéed garlic and onions to lamb. Pour broth or bouillon over lamb, garlic and onions. Cover and cook over medium-low heat 40 to 50 minutes or until tender, turning once. Remove lamb from skillet; place on a warm platter. In a small bowl, blend cornstarch and water. Stir cornstarch mixture into cooking juices. Bring to a boil, stirring until thickened. To serve, ladle thickened cooking juices over lamb. Makes 6 to 8 servings.

# Simple Lamb Stew

Gulasz Barani

*Really a lamb goulash.*

| | |
|---|---|
| 1/4 cup all-purpose flour | 2 medium onions, quartered |
| 1 teaspoon salt | 1 cup Chicken Broth, page 28, or bouillon |
| 1/4 teaspoon ground sweet paprika | 1 cup tomato paste |
| 1/8 teaspoon freshly ground black pepper | Cooked rice, if desired |
| 2 lbs. boneless lamb, cut in 3/4-inch cubes | Chopped fresh parsley |
| 2 tablespoons vegetable oil | |

Combine flour, salt, paprika and pepper in a small bowl. Place flour mixture in a shallow dish. Roll lamb in flour mixture; reserve remaining flour mixture. Heat oil in a large skillet. Add lamb; sauté over medium heat until evenly browned. Add onions. Reduce heat to low. Sauté until onions become partially tender. Add broth or bouillon. Cover and simmer 35 minutes, stirring occasionally. Stir in tomato paste. Simmer 20 minutes or until lamb is tender. Stir reserved flour mixture into lamb and cooking juices. Bring to a boil over medium heat until thickened. Serve hot, over rice, if desired. Garnish with parsley. Makes 6 servings.

# FISH &

A late December tradition that still exists at my home in northeastern Poland unfolds when my father brings home several live carp from market. Once home, he places the 3- to 4-pound fish in a tub filled with chilly well water that cleans every taint of silt or mud from the carp's system. Several days later, the still alive and healthy carp are passed into the care of my mother. She, however, is not so kind. She scales, dresses and more often than not prepares them in a variety of dishes.

In addition to carp, another fish commonly found in Polish lakes and rivers is the barracuda-like northern pike. Pike is most often fried, stuffed and baked, or simmered in a light broth.

One notable pike recipe is Stuffed Pike, in which the cavity of a 5- to 6-pound northern pike is filled with a stuffing of onions, celery, apples, mushrooms, croutons and parsley mixed with eggs. It's flavored with white wine, lemon juice and thyme.

Although carp and northern pike make up an important part of the Pole's non-meat diet, for sheer volume, no fish can approach the popularity enjoyed by the common herring. In Poland, you'll find herring of all sizes salted, pickled and marinated in oil. They're prepared in hot dishes, fried in omelets, batter-dipped or breaded and deep-fried, or simmered in broth and onions.

At least half the fish consumed in Poland is prepared as cold dishes. Several chilled-fish snacks appear in the appetizer chapter. Look for other cold fish recipes in the salad chapter. Many main dishes are also prepared cold, such as Cold Fillets in Vegetable Sauce, in which chunks of sautéed fillets are sprinkled with lemon juice, then refrigerated overnight in a sauce of tomato, onion, celery, carrot and parsley root.

Occasionally, frozen cod, haddock, ocean perch and other saltwater varieties are available in grocery stores in blocks of frozen fillets. These fillets are poached, boiled, steamed, fried, baked and sometimes broiled.

Regarding whole fresh fish, only the largest are filleted because the Polish cook believes that filleting results in excessive waste of meat and flavor in the smaller catches.

## Fried Fish

Smazona Ryba

*What could be easier than fresh fish, sizzling in a skillet?*

**2 lbs. small freshwater fish
   (perch, pike, trout), dressed
1-1/2 teaspoons salt
1/4 teaspoon freshly ground black pepper**

**1/4 cup all-purpose flour
1/2 cup vegetable oil
1 lemon, cut in wedges**

Rinse fish with cold water; pat dry with paper towels. Cut fish crosswise into 3-inch chunks. Sprinkle with salt and pepper. Place flour in a pie plate. Roll fish in flour until evenly coated. Heat oil in a large skillet over medium heat. Add floured fish; fry 7 to 8 minutes on each side or until fish is opaque throughout and flakes easily with a fork. Serve garnished with lemon wedges. Makes 6 servings.

# GAME

One January in Poland, after my husband emerged from the forest with a creel of fresh perch that had been caught through the ice, he decided to scale, fillet and fry them, Pennsylvania-style, for my family. I'll never forget how my mother watched aghast as he carried out his plans, and how on the sly she salvaged the discarded heads and bones. Later she made a delicious broth that my husband enjoyed, none the wiser.

Rabbit is the most accessible game meat in Poland. Even though hunting licenses—and the licenses needed to own and carry firearms—are too expensive for the average Pole, rabbits still find their way onto the typical family table. Rabbits are so common in Poland, and so simple to catch in homemade snares, that even young boys are sent into the forest to catch Sunday's main dish.

Rabbit is a sweet meat that tastes much like chicken. It can be fried, braised, boiled, stewed or used in practically any recipe that calls for chicken.

Young rabbits are most tender. Older rabbits tend to be tough and stringy. It's best to get rabbit in the fall or winter months when the meat is generally at its peak.

If your rabbit will come from a hunter relative or friend, have it skinned and dressed as soon as possible after it's killed. Scent glands located under the front legs where they join the body should be removed to avoid tainting the meat.

Soak rabbit overnight in salted water and a few tablespoons of vinegar to reduce any strong wild-game flavor that might be present. This is not necessary if using tame rabbit.

# Stuffed Pike   Photo on pages 126 & 127.

Szczupak Nadziewany

*Trout, salmon, carp or whitefish may also be prepared this way.*

1 teaspoon salt
1/2 teaspoon freshly ground black pepper
1/4 teaspoon ground sweet paprika
1 (5- to 6-lb.) dressed pike
1/2 cup butter or margarine
2 large onions, chopped
1 large celery root, shredded, or
   3 celery stalks, chopped
3 medium apples, peeled, chopped

1-1/2 tablespoons chopped fresh parsley
1 cup fresh mushrooms, minced
About 4-1/2 cups croutons
1-1/2 teaspoons sugar
1/2 teaspoon ground thyme
Juice of 1/2 lemon
3 eggs
About 2/3 cup white wine
3 tablespoons butter or margarine, melted

Combine salt, pepper and paprika in a small bowl. Rub salt mixture evenly over fish cavity. Cover; refrigerate 15 minutes. Preheat oven to 350F (175C). Grease a 13'' x 9'' baking dish. Melt 1/2 cup butter or margarine in a large skillet. Sauté onions and celery root or celery over medium heat until tender. Reduce heat to low. Add apples, parsley and mushrooms. Simmer, stirring until mushrooms become tender; remove from heat. Add 4-1/2 cups croutons, sugar, thyme, lemon juice, eggs and wine. Stir to combine. If stuffing mixture is too dry, add a little wine; if too moist, add a few more croutons. Cool. Loosely fill fish cavity with stuffing, allowing room for expansion during cooking. Place fish in greased dish. Bake 35 to 45 minutes or until fish is opaque throughout and flakes easily with a fork. Baste with melted butter or margarine about every 10 minutes. Serve immediately. Makes 8 to 10 servings.

# Fish Croquettes

Krokiety Rybne

*These tasty morsels will turn simple broth or bouillon into something special.*

1-1/2 lbs. fresh or thawed frozen
   fish fillets, skinned
1-1/2 slightly stale dinner rolls
1 cup milk
2 eggs

1 teaspoon salt
1/4 teaspoon white pepper
1 tablespoon chopped fresh parsley
3 to 4 qts. Chicken Broth, page 28,
   or bouillon

Using a grinder, grind fish into a medium bowl. In a small bowl, soak rolls in milk until absorbed. With your hands, squeeze excess milk from rolls. Grind squeezed rolls; add to fish along with eggs, salt, white pepper and parsley. Blend fish mixture. Wet your hands; form walnut-sized balls from fish mixture. Place each ball on a baking sheet. In a large saucepan, bring 2 to 2-1/2 quarts broth or bouillon to a boil over high heat. Gently drop fish balls into boiling liquid; bring back to a boil. Reduce heat to medium. Cook, uncovered, 8 to 10 minutes or until croquettes float. Cover with a tight-fitting lid. Cook 5 to 7 minutes or until a total of 15 minutes is reached. Remove croquettes with a slotted spoon; discard cooking liquid. Place croquettes on a platter. Serve with fresh hot broth or bouillon, if desired. Makes about 30 fish croquettes.

 *If fish mixture is very soft, add enough dry bread crumbs to bring mixture to a proper handling consistency.*

# Batter-Dipped Herring

Sledz Maczany w Ciescie

*To prepare these herring Polish-style, do not remove the bones before frying.*

| | |
|---|---|
| 2 lbs. salted dressed herring | 1/3 cup dairy sour cream |
| Vegetable oil | 1/4 cup all-purpose flour |
| 2 eggs, separated | Lemon wedges |
| 2 tablespoons olive oil | |

Cut herring in 2-1/2- to 3-inch pieces. Place herring in a large bowl with cold water to cover. Refrigerate 6 to 8 hours or overnight, changing water 3 times. Remove herring from water; pat dry. Pour oil 2 inches deep in a large saucepan. Heat to 350F (175C) or until a 1-inch bread cube turns golden brown in 65 seconds. In a medium bowl, beat egg yolks, olive oil, sour cream and flour until smooth. In a medium bowl, beat egg whites until stiff peaks form. Fold beaten egg whites into flour mixture until smooth. Dip herring in resulting batter. Let excess batter drip off. Gently place herring in hot oil. Deep-fry 5 to 6 minutes, turning once. Drain fish on paper towels. Serve hot with lemon wedges. Makes 6 servings.

# Broiled Fish Fillets

Zapiekana Ryba

*An elegant yet simple dish, perfect for entertaining.*

| | |
|---|---|
| 1-1/2 tablespoons butter or margarine | 1/4 cup dairy sour cream |
| 1/2 lb. fresh mushrooms, sliced | 1/2 cup shredded sharp Cheddar cheese |
| 1-1/2 lbs. fresh fish fillets |   (2 oz.) |
| Juice of 1/2 lemon | Ground sweet paprika |
| 1/2 teaspoon salt | 2 tablespoons dry bread crumbs |

Melt butter or margarine in a medium skillet. Add sliced mushrooms; sauté over medium heat until tender and liquid evaporates. Preheat broiler. Grease a large, shallow baking dish. Arrange fillets in greased dish. Sprinkle with lemon juice and salt. Broil 5 minutes. Spoon sautéed mushrooms over fillets. Spoon sour cream over mushrooms. Top with cheese, paprika to taste and bread crumbs. Broil 5 to 8 minutes or until fish is opaque throughout and flakes easily with a fork. Makes 4 to 6 servings.

# How to Make Fish in Aspic

1/Arrange a few carrot slices, lemon slices, egg wedges and parsley sprigs over set aspic.

2/Arrange fish pieces over aspic. Gently pour more aspic over fish. Cover and refrigerate until set.

# Fish in Aspic

Ryba w Galarecie

*A cool, colorful fish dish, perfect to serve at a buffet or special luncheon.*

**4 cups Vegetable Broth, page 28,**
  **or chicken bouillon**
**2 lbs. dressed pike, carp or trout**
**5 black peppercorns**
**2 bay leaves**
**10 capers**
**1-1/2 tablespoons unflavored gelatin powder**

**3 tablespoons cold water**
**1 large carrot, thinly sliced**
**1/2 lemon, thinly sliced**
**4 hard-cooked eggs, cut in wedges**
**Fresh parsley sprigs**
**Fresh lettuce or spinach**

Heat broth or bouillon in a medium saucepan. Cut fish into 2-inch pieces. Add fish, peppercorns, bay leaves and capers to hot broth or bouillon. Simmer, partially covered, over low heat 20 to 30 minutes or until fish is opaque throughout and easily flakes with a fork. Remove fish from cooking liquid. Strain liquid into a medium bowl. In a small bowl, dissolve gelatin in water. Stir into strained liquid; let cool slightly. Pour a thin layer of aspic into a deep, 2-quart casserole or 3-inch-deep loaf dish. Refrigerate until set. Arrange a few carrot slices, lemon slices, egg wedges and parsley over set aspic; top with a small amount of liquid aspic. Refrigerate until set. Arrange fish pieces over aspic. Gently pour remaining aspic over fish. Cover and refrigerate until set. Line a large platter with fresh lettuce or spinach. To serve, dip casserole or loaf dish in hot water several seconds. Invert aspic onto lined platter. Serve chilled. Makes 6 to 8 servings.

Fish in Aspic

# How to Make Cold Fillets in Vegetable Sauce

1/Place flour in a shallow dish. Roll fillets in flour until evenly coated; shake off excess.

2/Place cooked fish in a baking dish. Sprinkle with lemon juice. Spoon cooked vegetable mixture over fish.

## Cold Fillets in Vegetable Sauce

Ryba na Zimno w Sosie Warzywnym

*In Poland, fresh carp is often used as the main ingredient in this tasty appetizer.*

**1-1/2 lbs. fresh fish fillets, skinned**
**3/4 cup plus 2 tablespoons vegetable oil**
**1/2 teaspoon salt**
**2 small onions, minced**
**1/2 celery root, shredded**
**2 medium carrots, shredded**
**1 leek, thinly sliced**

**1 parsley root, shredded**
**3 tablespoons tomato paste**
**1/4 cup Chicken Broth, page 28, or bouillon**
**1/8 teaspoon freshly ground black pepper**
**1/2 teaspoon sugar**
**1/3 cup all-purpose flour**
**Juice of 1/2 lemon**

Cut fillets into 3-inch pieces; set aside. In a medium saucepan, combine 3/4 cup oil, salt, onions, celery root, carrots, leek and parsley root. Cook, uncovered, over medium-low heat 15 to 20 minutes or until vegetables are tender. In a small bowl, blend tomato paste and broth or bouillon. Stir into vegetables. Cook 15 minutes over medium-low heat, stirring occasionally. Season with pepper and sugar. Heat 2 tablespoons oil in a large skillet. Place flour in a shallow dish. Roll fish pieces in flour until evenly coated; shake off excess. Add floured fish pieces to skillet. Fry over medium-high heat 4 to 6 minutes on each side or until fish is opaque throughout and flakes easily with a fork. Carefully place fish in a medium baking dish. Sprinkle with lemon juice. Spoon cooked vegetable mixture over fish. Let cool. Cover and refrigerate overnight. Serve chilled. Makes 10 to 12 servings.

# Broiled Fillets

Zapiekane Filety

*Serve these tender fish fillets with boiled potatoes and Fisherman's Salad, page 51.*

| | |
|---|---|
| **6 freshwater fish fillets (about 2 lbs.)** | **2 tablespoons vegetable oil** |
| **Juice of 1/2 lemon** | **2 tablespoons butter or margarine,** |
| **Salt** | **room temperature** |
| **Freshly ground black pepper** | **2 tablespoons grated Parmesan cheese** |
| **Dried-leaf Italian seasoning** | **1/3 cup dairy sour cream** |

Arrange fillets, skin-side down, in a shallow dish. Sprinkle with lemon juice, salt, pepper and Italian seasoning to taste. Let stand 15 minutes. Preheat broiler. Lightly grease a baking dish. Heat oil in a large skillet. Place fillets, skin-side down, in skillet. Cook over medium heat 3 to 4 minutes. Turn and cook 2 minutes. Place fillets in greased dish, skin-side down. Dab 1 teaspoon butter or margarine on each fillet; top with cheese. Broil fish 2 minutes. Spread sour cream evenly over fillets. Broil 5 minutes or until fish is opaque throughout and flakes easily with a fork. Makes 6 servings.

# Tartar Sauce

Sos Tatarski

*Adding pickled mushrooms makes this tasty version of tartar sauce truly unique.*

| | |
|---|---|
| **1-1/8 cups Mayonnaise, page 53,** | **1/4 cup pickled mushrooms, diced** |
| **or other mayonnaise** | **1 teaspoon minced onion** |
| **2 medium dill pickles, peeled, diced** | **1 teaspoon prepared mustard** |

Combine all ingredients in a medium bowl. Cover and refrigerate 30 minutes. Makes about 1-1/2 cups.

# Baked Rabbit

Zajac

*Although it takes a long time to prepare, this tasty recipe is really quite simple.*

| | |
|---|---|
| **1 cup vinegar** | **1/4 lb. fresh bacon slices** |
| **1 bay leaf** | **1 cup dairy sour cream** |
| **10 black peppercorns** | **1 tablespoon all-purpose flour** |
| **1 (4- to 4-1/2-lb.) rabbit, cut up** | |

Place vinegar, bay leaf and peppercorns in a small saucepan. Bring to a boil over medium heat. Reduce heat to low. Simmer 15 minutes. Let cool. Place rabbit pieces in a shallow baking dish. Pour vinegar mixture over rabbit. Cover and refrigerate 12 to 24 hours, turning occasionally. Preheat oven to 350F (175C). Remove rabbit from marinade; pat dry. Wrap rabbit pieces with bacon slices by stretching bacon around rabbit and securing with wooden picks. Return wrapped rabbit to marinade. Bake, uncovered, 45 minutes or until tender, turning once. Combine sour cream and flour in a small bowl. Spoon sour-cream mixture over rabbit. Bake 15 minutes. Makes 4 servings.

# BEEF &

There's a saying in Poland: "Years ago, when you went into a shop that said *Butcher* over its doors, you found meat inside. Today, you enter a shop that says *Meat,* and you find a butcher."

That saying applies to beef, above all. In Poland, a strip, sirloin or porterhouse steak is all but unheard of, a rare thing indeed. Beef is available from time to time, but only in the poorest of cuts. The best steaks and roasts somehow seem to find their way out of the country. Beef cuts that remain are roasts, lean cuts like flank steak and, once in a while, beef round. But mostly there's ground beef and beef bones.

This is not to say that beef doesn't have its niche in Polish cooking. It has. Beef bones and scraps have flavored many a rich broth traditionally used as a base for important dishes like Flaki, or Polish Tripe Soup.

Ground beef is prepared into Beef Patties, and various fillings for pierogies and other recipes. When combined with ground pork, it rallies into a delicious Meat Loaf with Eggs.

Slices of lean beef often are tenderized with a meat mallet, then rolled jelly-roll style along with vegetable or other filling mixtures. The rolls are simmered in a flavorful beef broth thickened with a flour and butter or sour-cream mixture.

Beef is also cooked slowly with mushrooms and vegetables, into a dish resembling Swiss steak. In this case, it's called Sosnowiec Steak, named after the Polish town that devised this simple recipe. In bite-sized pieces, beef is combined with similar chunks of pork to make the Polish version of Hungarian Goulash. This is served hot over potato pancakes, noodles or rice.

Then there's a special, once-a-year roast beef, stuffed with a sweet red-onion filling in deep pockets, carved so each moist slice contains a flavorful helping of onions.

Beef liver—more available than beef—is usually sautéed with onion rings and simmered in wine.

Veal is the third most common meat in Poland, far behind chicken and pork, and slightly ahead of beef. The Poles like its delicate, mild flavor, and the way it easily accepts the flavors of any herbs or seasonings it's cooked with. But the wise

## Veal & Eggs

Cielecina z Jajkami

*A mild-flavored breakfast dish popular during the fall.*

1/4 cup butter or margarine
3 cups chopped cooked veal
1 medium onion, chopped
2 garlic cloves, minced

1 teaspoon salt
1/4 teaspoon freshly ground black pepper
8 eggs

Melt 2 tablespoons butter or margarine in a large skillet. Add veal, onion, garlic, salt and pepper. Sauté over medium heat until onions are tender. Add remaining 2 tablespoons butter or margarine. In a medium bowl, lightly beat eggs with a fork. Stir into sautéed veal mixture. Reduce heat to medium-low. Cook, gently stirring, until eggs set but are still moist. Remove from heat. Serve immediately. Makes 6 servings.

# VEAL

cook also knows that there's little marbling or fat in the young white to light-pink meat, and if not carefully watched, veal can easily be dried out during cooking.

If the best cuts of beef are exported, then what of veal? If it's not readily available in stores, then where does the population find it?

Many families living on small or large farms, or even in homes on the outskirts of large towns and cities, own at least one milk cow. That being the case, there's usually one enterprising individual in the area who keeps several bulls that do little else than service all of the milk cows for miles around. The milk cows bear calves, which helps perpetuate their milk-producing abilities and also provides a source of fresh veal.

Veal in Poland is prepared in a manner similar to pork. Boneless slices of veal leg or loin are pounded with a meat mallet or flat side of a cleaver. They're braised, breaded and sautéed, used for cutlets or stuffed and rolled, as in Veal Rollups. Here, tenderized veal is seasoned, rolled up around slices of bacon, sautéed with onions and simmered in a mixture of chicken broth, tomatoes and seasoning thickened with sour cream and flour.

Pocket Veal Roast is a unique roast variation. A boneless veal roast is prepared by cutting pockets and inserting folded bacon slices in each pocket. Chopped zucchini arranged around the roast helps make the cooking juices something special to be strained and served hot over carved slices of moist, tender veal.

# Pocket Veal Roast

Pieczen z Cieleciny Nadziewana

*The delicate flavor of veal complements the fresh taste of lemon and zucchini in this no-waste main dish.*

1 (3- to 3-1/2-lb.) boneless rolled veal
   shoulder or rump roast, tied with string
10 to 12 bacon slices
1 cup Chicken Broth, page 28, or bouillon
1 tablespoon butter or margarine, melted
Juice of 1/2 lemon

1 teaspoon salt
1 tablespoon freshly grated lemon peel
2 anchovy fillets, drained and minced
1 tablespoon dry bread crumbs
1 medium zucchini, chopped

Preheat oven to 350F (175C). With a sharp knife, cut 10 to 12 (2-inch) pockets in veal, evenly spaced over top and sides of roast. Insert 1 folded bacon slice in each pocket. Place veal on a rack in a roasting pan. Sprinkle top of veal with broth or bouillon, melted butter or margarine, lemon juice, salt, lemon peel and anchovies. Top with bread crumbs. Place zucchini around bottom of roast. Cover with a tight-fitting lid. Roast 1-1/2 to 2 hours or until tender. Remove roast and let stand, covered, 15 minutes. Strain cooking juices into a serving bowl; reserve zucchini. Slice roast; arrange slices on a warm platter. Serve with strained cooking juices and cooked zucchini, if desired. Makes 6 to 8 servings.

# Veal Paprika

Paprykarz Cielecy

*A great way to spice up the mild flavor of veal.*

2 to 2-1/2 lbs. veal
1/4 cup plus 1 tablespoon all-purpose flour
2 tablespoons vegetable oil
2 large onions, minced
1 tablespoon ground sweet paprika

1/2 cup Chicken Broth, page 28, or bouillon
1/2 cup dairy sour cream
1 teaspoon salt
Juice from 1/2 lemon
Hot cooked white rice

Cut veal into bite-sized pieces. Place 1/4 cup flour and veal pieces in a heavy plastic bag; shake to coat with flour. Heat oil in a large skillet. Add veal; sauté over medium heat until browned on all sides. Add onions; sprinkle with paprika. Pour broth or bouillon into skillet. Cover and cook over medium-low heat 30 minutes or until veal is tender, stirring occasionally. In a small bowl, combine sour cream and 1 tablespoon flour. Stir sour-cream mixture into veal and cooking juices. Cook until juices are slightly thickened; do not boil. Season with salt and lemon juice. Serve hot over rice. Makes 6 to 8 servings.

# How to Make Pocket Veal Roast

1/With a sharp knife, cut 10 to 12 (2-inch) pockets in veal, evenly spaced over top and sides of roast.

2/Fold each bacon slice into a small square. Insert 1 folded bacon slice into each pocket.

# Veal Rollups

Zrazy Cielece

*These delicate rollups will provide your guests with a tasty, light dinner.*

| | |
|---|---|
| 2 to 2-1/2 lbs. boneless veal | 8 medium tomatoes, peeled, sliced |
| Freshly ground black pepper | 1 teaspoon salt |
| 12 bacon slices | 1/2 teaspoon sugar |
| About 1-1/2 tablespoons all-purpose flour | 1/2 teaspoon ground sweet paprika |
| 2 tablespoons vegetable oil | 2 tablespoons all-purpose flour |
| 1 large onion, halved, sliced | 3 tablespoons dairy sour cream |
| 1 cup Chicken Broth, page 28, or bouillon | Fresh chopped parsley |

Cut veal into 12 (1/2-inch-thick) pieces; place between plastic wrap. Using a meat mallet, pound each piece until 1/8 inch thick. Sprinkle with pepper. Place 1 bacon slice on each piece of veal. Roll jelly-roll style. Secure with wooden picks. Evenly sprinkle veal rolls with flour. Heat oil in a large skillet. Add onion and veal rolls; sauté over medium heat until browned on all sides. Heat broth or bouillon in a large saucepan. Add onion and browned veal rolls. Cover and simmer 15 minutes. Add tomatoes, salt, 1/2 teaspoon pepper, sugar and paprika. Cover and simmer 20 minutes. In a small bowl, combine flour and sour cream. Stir flour mixture into simmering veal rolls and cooking juices. Increase heat to medium. Cook until slightly thickened, stirring frequently. To serve, arrange veal rolls on a warm platter. Top with hot cooking juices and tomatoes. Garnish with parsley. Serve immediately. Makes 6 servings.

# Pan-Braised Veal

Cielecina Duszona

*Serve this dish with boiled young potatoes sprinkled with parsley, and buttered green peas and onions.*

| | |
|---|---|
| **2-1/2 lbs. veal** | **1 teaspoon salt** |
| **1 teaspoon freshly ground black pepper** | **3 tablespoons dry bread crumbs** |
| **2 tablespoons butter or margarine** | **1/2 cup Chicken Broth, page 28, or bouillon** |
| **Juice of 1 lemon** | |

Cut veal into 6 equal pieces about 1/2 inch thick. Place each veal piece between plastic wrap. Using a meat mallet, until 1/4 inch thick. Sprinkle both sides with pepper. Melt butter or margarine in a large skillet. Add veal; sauté over medium heat 3 to 4 minutes on each side or until browned. Reduce heat to medium-low. Sprinkle lemon juice, salt and bread crumbs on veal. Add broth or bouillon to skillet. Cover and cook over medium-low heat 40 to 45 minutes or until tender, occasionally basting with cooking juices. Be careful not to wash bread crumbs from veal with baste. Serve hot. Makes 6 servings.

# Polish Beef

Wolowina po Polsku

*Maggi seasoning is the Polish equivalent of soy sauce, available in most supermarkets.*

| | |
|---|---|
| **2-1/2 to 3 lbs. beef round steak,** | **2 tablespoons butter or margarine** |
| **cut 1 inch thick** | **2 medium onions, halved, sliced** |
| **1-1/4 cups red wine** | **1 lb. fresh mushrooms, sliced** |
| **5 tablespoons vegetable oil** | **All-purpose flour** |
| **1 teaspoon Maggi seasoning** | **1 tablespoon cornstarch** |
| **1 tablespoon salt** | **2 tablespoons water** |
| **1 teaspoon freshly ground black pepper** | |

Cut beef into oval pieces (5'' x 3''). Using a meat mallet, pound meat until about 1/2 inch thick. In a shallow 9- or 10-inch-square baking dish, combine wine, 2 tablespoons oil, Maggi seasoning, salt and pepper. Place meat in marinade. Refrigerate 1 hour, turning meat every 15 minutes. Melt butter or margarine in a medium skillet. Add onions; sauté until tender. Remove meat from marinade; place in a medium bowl. Pour marinade into a large skillet. Add mushrooms. Cook, uncovered, over medium heat until tender, about 5 to 7 minutes. Add sautéed onions. Cook 5 minutes over medium-low heat. Place meat on a flat working surface. Evenly sprinkle flour on both sides of meat. Place on a rack. Let stand 5 minutes. Preheat oven to 350F (175C). Heat remaining 3 tablespoons oil in a large skillet. Add meat; sauté over medium-high heat until browned. Arrange meat in a 9- or 10-inch-square baking dish. Spoon onions, mushrooms and juice over meat. Cover with foil or a tight-fitting lid. Bake 30 minutes or until tender. Remove from oven. Remove meat pieces to a warm platter and keep warm; reserve juices. In a small bowl, blend cornstarch and water. Stir into onion mixture. Cook over medium heat until slightly thickened. Pour over meat. Serve hot. Makes 6 servings.

# Marinated Beef Roast

Marynowana Pieczen Wolowa

*Leftovers of this roast make an excellent pierogi filling.*

**Marinade, see below**
**1 (3-lb.) lean boneless beef chuck roast**
**Salt**
**1/2 teaspoon ground sweet paprika**

**2 tablespoons vegetable oil**
**1/2 pint dairy sour cream (1 cup)**
**1 tablespoon all-purpose flour**

*Marinade:*
**2 cups dry red wine**
**Juice from 1-1/2 lemons**
**1/4 cup water**
**2 medium onions, quartered**
**1 carrot, quartered**

**1 parsley root, halved**
**1/2 celery root**
**10 black peppercorns**
**1/4 teaspoon ground thyme**
**1 bay leaf**

Prepare Marinade. Place roast in a small, deep, non-metallic, baking dish. Add hot marinade; cool, then cover with plastic wrap or foil. Refrigerate 2 days, turning roast twice per day. Remove meat from marinade; reserve marinade. Pat roast dry. Rub with salt. Sprinkle roast with paprika. Preheat oven to 325F (165C). Heat oil in a medium skillet. Add roast; brown on all sides over medium-high heat. Transfer roast to a small, deep baking dish. Add reserved marinade. Cover and cook 2 hours, basting with marinade every 15 minutes. In a small bowl, combine sour cream and flour until smooth. Spoon resulting mixture evenly over meat. Bake, uncovered, 15 to 20 minutes or until glaze forms and meat is tender. To serve, remove roast. Slice; place on a serving dish. Strain marinade; ladle over meat. Makes 6 servings.

**Marinade:**
Combine all ingredients in a medium saucepan. Bring to a boil over medium heat. Boil 1 to 2 minutes.

# Beef Liver & Onions

Watrobka Wolowa z Cebulka

*For a sweeter dish, try red onions.*

**1/4 cup all-purpose flour**
**1-1/2 lbs. sliced beef liver**
**1/4 cup butter or margarine**
**4 medium onions, sliced,**
  **separated into rings**

**Salt**
**Freshly ground black pepper**
**1 cup dry red wine**
**1 tablespoon cornstarch, if desired**
**1 tablespoon water, if desired**

Place flour in a shallow dish. Dip liver in flour until evenly coated. Melt butter or margarine in a large skillet. Add onions; sauté over medium-low heat until tender. Remove onions from cooking juices. Add floured liver slices to skillet; sauté over medium heat 4 to 5 minutes on each side or until evenly browned. Sprinkle with salt and pepper to taste. Pour wine into skillet. Cover with a tight-fitting lid. Cook over medium-low heat, 8 to 10 minutes or until liver is tender. Serve hot. If desired, thicken cooking juices with a mixture of cornstarch and water. Makes 4 to 6 servings.

# How to Make Roast Beef with Onion Stuffing

1/Cut whole onions in 1/4-inch-thick slices. Impale whole onion slices on wooden picks inserted in the roast, pressing slices against top and side of roast.

2/With a sharp knife, cut 6 to 8 deep pockets across the width of the roast at 1- to 1-1/4-inch intervals, being careful not to cut through side or bottom. Spoon Onion Stuffing into each pocket.

# Hungarian Goulash

Wegierski Gulasz

*Traditionally served over potatoes or noodles, also excellent with Potato Pancakes, page 62.*

| | |
|---|---|
| 1-1/2 lbs. lean beef, pork or veal | 2 medium green bell peppers, |
| 2 tablespoons vegetable oil | sliced into 1/2-inch strips |
| 2 medium onions, chopped | 2 medium tomatoes, cut into wedges, or |
| 2 cups Beef Broth, page 27; | 1 tablespoon tomato paste |
| Meat Broth, page 27; or bouillon | 1 cup red wine |
| 1/2 teaspoon ground sweet paprika | 1/4 cup water |
| 1/4 teaspoon freshly ground black pepper | 1 tablespoon cornstarch |
| 1/4 teaspoon ground marjoram | 1/4 teaspoon salt |

Cut beef, pork or veal into 1/2- to 3/4-inch cubes. Heat oil in a large skillet. Add meat and onions; sauté over medium-high heat until meat browns on all sides. Place browned meat and onions in a medium saucepan. Add broth or bouillon, paprika, black pepper and marjoram. Cover and cook over medium heat 50 minutes. Add green peppers and tomatoes or tomato paste. Stir gently. Cover and cook 10 minutes. Add wine. Cover and simmer over low heat 10 minutes. In a small cup, blend water and cornstarch until smooth. Stir into meat mixture. Season with salt. Bring to a boil, stirring until slightly thickened. Serve hot over potatoes, potato pancakes, noodles or rice. Makes 6 to 8 servings.

On preceding page, Christmas Eve medley, clockwise from top center: Red-Cabbage Salad, page 44; Fancy Fruitcake, page 138; Honey-Walnut Mazurka, page 150; Poppy-Seed Roll, page 146; Sauerkraut-Filled Pierogies, page 81; Stuffed Pike, page 114; Marinated Herring, page 20; Christmas Eve Borscht, page 37; and Dried-Mushroom Soup, page 30, served with Mushroom-Filled Ravioli, page 83.

# Roast Beef with Onion Stuffing

Pieczen Wolowa z Cebulowym Nadzieniem

*Select fresh sweet red onions for the stuffing.*

**Onion Stuffing, see below**
**1 tablespoon butter or margarine**
**1 (4- to 4-1/2-lb.) rolled beef round or**
   **rump roast**
**1 teaspoon salt**
**2 medium onions, sliced 1/4 inch thick**

**1/2 oz. dried mushrooms**
**8 black peppercorns**
**2 bay leaves**
**1-1/2 cups Meat Broth, page 27, or bouillon**
**All-purpose flour**

*Onion Stuffing:*
**2 tablespoons butter or margarine**
**2 medium onions, minced**

**1/4 cup minced celery**
**3 tablespoons dry bread crumbs**

Prepare Onion Stuffing. Preheat oven to 325F (165C). Melt butter or margarine in a large skillet. Sauté meat over medium-high heat, 5 to 7 minutes, turning until browned on all sides. Place in a medium roasting pan. Pour cooking juices over meat. Sprinkle with salt. Impale whole onion slices on wooden picks, pressing slices against top and side of roast. Wash mushrooms. Arrange in pan around roast. Add peppercorns, bay leaves and 1 cup broth or bouillon. Cover and bake 1-1/2 hours or until nearly tender. Baste roast with some of remaining 1/2 cup broth or bouillon every 15 to 20 minutes until all remaining broth or bouillon is used. Remove from oven. Cool 10 minutes. Remove onion slices and wooden picks; discard. With a sharp knife, cut 6 to 8 deep pockets across the width of roast at 1- to 1-1/4-inch intervals, being careful not to cut through sides or bottom. Spoon Onion Stuffing into each pocket. Sprinkle a little flour over top of roast. Bake, uncovered, 30 minutes or until tender. Before serving, slice roast between pockets, so each serving contains stuffing. Serve hot on a platter, with pan juices, if desired. Makes 8 servings.

**Onion Stuffing:**
In a medium skillet, melt butter or margarine. Add onions, celery and bread crumbs; sauté over medium heat until onions are tender. Let cool.

# Ground-Beef Patties

Kotlety Wolowe

*This dish is a favorite of Poles everywhere.*

**1-1/2 lbs. lean ground beef**
**2/3 cup dry bread crumbs**
**3/4 cup milk**
**1 egg, beaten**
**1 medium onion, minced**

**1/2 teaspoon ground sweet paprika**
**1/2 teaspoon salt**
**1/2 teaspoon freshly ground black pepper**
**1/4 teaspoon garlic salt**
**3 tablespoons vegetable oil**

In a large bowl, combine ground beef, 1/2 cup bread crumbs, milk, egg, onion, paprika, salt, pepper and garlic salt. Shape beef mixture into patties. Lightly press both sides of each patty in remaining bread crumbs. Heat oil in a large skillet; sauté patties over medium heat, 3 to 4 minutes on each side or until browned and cooked to desired doneness. Serve hot. Makes 4 to 6 servings.

# Sosnowiec Steak

Zrazy z Sosnowca

*This dish tastes like fancy Swiss Steak.*

6 (1/2-inch-thick) pieces lean beef
   round steak (about 1-1/2 lbs.)
1/4 cup vegetable oil
2 medium onions, sliced
2 cups fresh mushrooms or
   1 cup rehydrated dried mushrooms

1/2 cup dry red wine
2-1/4 cups water
6 medium baking potatoes, peeled
1-1/2 teaspoons Maggi seasoning
Pinch of salt
1 tablespoon cornstarch

Place steaks between plastic wrap. Using a meat mallet, pound steaks about 5 times on each side. Heat oil in a large skillet. Sauté steak over medium-high heat about 10 minutes or until browned. Transfer meat to another large skillet. Place onions in same skillet used to sauté steak; sauté over medium heat until tender, 3 to 5 minutes. Add to steak. If using rehydrated mushrooms, add to steak without sautéing. Place fresh mushrooms in remaining steak and onion juices. Sauté over medium heat 5 minutes or until tender. Add to steak. Add wine and 2 cups water to steak. Cover and simmer 30 minutes. Slice potatoes into crescent-shaped pieces. Add sliced potatoes, Maggi seasoning and salt. Cover and cook 30 minutes over medium-low heat so juice does not bubble. In a small bowl, blend 1/4 cup cold water and cornstarch until smooth. Gently stir into steak mixture. Cover; simmer 10 minutes over low heat or until slightly thickened. Serve hot. Makes 6 servings.

# Meat Loaf with Eggs

Klops Nadziewany Jajami

*Excellent served hot as a main dish, or cold as a sandwich filling.*

About 2 cups dry bread crumbs
3/4 cup milk
2 tablespoons butter or margarine
2 medium onions, minced
2 lbs. lean ground beef
1-1/2 lbs. lean ground pork

1/2 teaspoon garlic powder
1-1/2 teaspoons salt
1 teaspoon freshly ground black pepper
2 eggs, beaten
1/4 cup chopped fresh parsley
3 hard-cooked eggs, halved lengthwise

Preheat oven to 350F (175C). In a small bowl, soak 1-1/2 cups bread crumbs in milk. Melt butter or margarine in a medium skillet over medium-high heat. Add onions; sauté 5 minutes or until soft. In a large bowl, mix beef and pork. Add soaked bread crumbs, sautéed onions, garlic powder, salt, pepper and beaten eggs; mix thoroughly. On a large cutting board, sprinkle remaining 1/2 cup bread crumbs evenly over a 13" x 12" rectangular area. Pat meat mixture over bread crumbs, using your hands or the flat side of a knife blade. Form meat into a 13" x 12" rectangle, about 1 inch thick. Sprinkle 2 tablespoons parsley over a 1-inch-wide strip of meat mixture, about 3 inches in from 1 long side. Arrange halves of hard-cooked eggs, lengthwise, cut-sides down, on top of parsley strip. Lightly press eggs into meat. Sprinkle remaining parsley over eggs. Roll meat, jelly-roll style, starting from long side closest to eggs, so eggs end up in center of meat loaf. When finished rolling, pat meat loaf ends until rounded. Grease a deep 13" x 9" baking dish. Place meat loaf, seam-side down, in pan. Bake, uncovered, 1-1/2 hours or until done. Makes 10 to 12 servings.

# Party Beef Rolls

Zrazy Wolowe

*Use these beef rolls for parties and special buffets.*

2 to 2-1/2 lbs. beef round steak,
   sliced 1/2 inch thick
1-3/4 cups Beef Broth, page 27, or bouillon
5 black peppercorns
1 bay leaf
5 tablespoons butter or margarine
1 medium onion, sliced, separated into rings

1/2 lb. fresh mushrooms, sliced
1/2 cup all-purpose flour
1/4 teaspoon freshly ground black pepper
1 teaspoon salt
1 tablespoon cornstarch
1 teaspoon Maggi seasoning

Place steaks between plastic wrap. Using a meat mallet, pound to approximately 6" x 4" ovals, 1/4 inch thick. In a medium saucepan, combine 1-1/2 cups broth or bouillon, peppercorns and bay leaf. Bring to a boil. Reduce heat to low. Simmer 10 minutes. Melt 1 tablespoon butter or margarine in a medium skillet. Add onion; sauté over medium heat until tender. Place beef ovals on a flat working surface. Place equal amounts of sautéed onion on 1 end of each beef roll, widthwise. Roll beef rolls jelly-roll style. Secure with wooden picks. Melt 2 tablespoons butter or margarine in same skillet. Add mushrooms; sauté over medium heat until tender. Add to simmering broth mixture. In a small bowl, combine flour, pepper and salt. Roll beef rolls in flour mixture. Melt remaining 2 tablespoons butter or margarine in same skillet. Add floured beef rolls; sauté over medium-high heat 4 to 5 minutes or until evenly browned. Place browned beef rolls in broth or bouillon mixture. Cover with a tight-fitting lid; simmer over low heat 1 to 1-1/2 hours or until tender. In a small bowl, blend cornstarch, Maggi seasoning and remaining 1/4 cup broth or bouillon. Add to beef rolls. Bring to a boil. Simmer 5 minutes. Serve immediately. Makes 6 to 8 servings.

# Browned Beef

Befsztyk

*An old stand-by Polish recipe prepared when beef is available.*

2 lbs. beef top-round steak, 1/2 inch thick
1/2 cup plus 1 tablespoon all-purpose flour
1/4 cup butter or margarine
2 medium onions, sliced

Salt
Freshly ground black pepper
1 cup Beef Broth, page 27, or bouillon

Slice beef into serving pieces. Place 1/2 cup flour in a shallow dish. Dip beef in flour until evenly coated. Melt 2 tablespoons butter or margarine in a large skillet. Add floured beef; sauté over medium heat until both sides are browned. Remove beef from skillet; set aside. Preheat oven to 325F (165C). Place onions in beef cooking juices. Sauté over medium heat until tender. Grease a 9- or 10-inch-square baking dish. Arrange sautéed onions in baking dish. Place beef on onions. Sprinkle with salt and pepper to taste. Pour broth or bouillon into baking dish. Cover with a tight-fitting lid. Bake 1 hour or until tender. Remove beef from baking dish; place on a hot platter. Strain and degrease cooking juices. Melt remaining 2 tablespoons butter or margarine in a small skillet. Add remaining 1 tablespoon flour; stir over medium-low heat until golden brown. In a small saucepan, combine flour mixture and cooking juices. Cook over medium heat, stirring constantly, until thickened. Serve resulting gravy over beef. Makes 6 servings.

# Beef Roll

Rolady Wolowe

*The broth used to prepare these versatile rolls can also be the main ingredient of a delicious gravy.*

2 (1- to 1-1/2-lb.) beef top-round steaks
1/2 teaspoon salt
1/2 teaspoon freshly ground black pepper
1/2 cup milk
1 cup soft bread crumbs
3 eggs
2 hard-cooked eggs, coarsely chopped

1 lb. lean ground beef
1/4 cup chopped fresh parsley
1/4 teaspoon dried leaf marjoram
1/4 teaspoon garlic powder
6 cups Beef Broth, page 27, or bouillon
3 tablespoons butter or margarine

Place each steak between plastic wrap. Using a meat mallet, pound each to a rectangle about 12''  x 8'' and 1/4 to 3/8 inch thick. When pounding meat, do not use a straight up-and-down movement. Use a sliding action to stretch meat more than flatten. Sprinkle 1/8 teaspoon salt and 1/8 teaspoon pepper on inner side of each steak. Roll each steak tightly. In a medium bowl, combine milk, bread crumbs, 2 eggs, hard-cooked eggs, ground beef, parsley, marjoram, garlic powder and remaining salt and pepper. Unroll steak rectangles. In a small bowl, beat 1 egg with a fork. Brush egg over inner side of each steak. Pat 1/2 of filling on each steak, making an even layer to within 1 inch from edges. Roll steaks tightly, lengthwise or widthwise, according to preference. Secure with wooden picks. In a large pot, boil broth or bouillon. Place each beef roll on a 20'' x 16'' piece of cheesecloth. Tightly roll each beef roll in cheesecloth. Tie ends closed with string. Wrap string several times along length of beef rolls. Place beef rolls in broth or bouillon. Cook, covered, over medium-high heat 1 hour. If broth or bouillon does not cover beef rolls, turn rolls every 15 minutes. Remove from broth or bouillon. Unwrap cheesecloth. In a large skillet, melt butter or margarine. Brown beef rolls over medium-high heat, about 5 minutes. Slice and serve with gravy, if desired. Makes 6 servings.

## Variation

To serve cold, remove from broth or bouillon. Let cool. When cool, cover and refrigerate overnight. Unwrap cheesecloth. Slice 3/8 inch thick. Serve as an appetizer or sandwich filling.

# How to Make Beef Roll

1/Place each steak between plastic wrap. Pound each to approximately 12" x 8". When pounding meat, do not use a straight up-and-down movement. Use a sliding action to stretch meat more than flatten.

2/Prepare filling mixture. Pat 1/2 of filling on each pounded steak, making an even layer. Roll each steak tightly, lengthwise or widthwise, according to preference.

3/Secure beef roll with wooden picks. Place each roll on cheesecloth. Tightly enclose each roll in cheesecloth. Tie ends with string. Wrap string several times around rolls.

4/To serve cold, remove from cooking liquid. When cool, cover and refrigerate overnight. Unwrap cheesecloth. Slice beef rolls 3/8 inch thick. Serve as an appetizer or sandwich filling.

# DESSERTS

It's a good thing that the dessert chapter is last. Otherwise, the rest of this book might never have been written.

The list of Polish desserts, it seems, goes on forever—and with good reason: Polish pastries and desserts take a back seat to no others in the world. Indeed, if the Polish cook can be said to be deadly serious about anything—he or she is serious about desserts.

Here are cheesecakes, ice creams and gelatin desserts. Also round jam-filled, powdered-sugar-dusted doughnuts called *paczki* (PONCH-kee); creamy-frosted multi-layered tortes; and mazurkas—frosted fruit and sugar-covered cookie crusts.

Within this chapter, you'll find cakes and rolls featuring poppy seeds and walnuts, spice cakes, and the photogenic Pyramid and Sculpture Cakes. You'll find airlike Cookie Crisps that simply melt in your mouth.

Yes, the dessert chapter has the largest number of recipes in the book—and the shortest introduction: *short and sweet.* Suffice to say that occasions are thought up in Poland, just so desserts can be served. Let the recipes speak for themselves! Onward, to desserts.

## Strawberry Dessert

Krem Smietankowy z Truskawkami

*A delightful dessert when strawberries are in their peak season.*

| | |
|---|---|
| 2 tablespoons unflavored gelatin powder | 2 tablespoons Vanilla Sugar, page 136 |
| 2 tablespoons cold water | 3 egg whites |
| 1 tablespoon boiling water | 1 pint fresh strawberries |
| 1-1/8 cups sweetened condensed milk | 2 oz. semisweet chocolate curls |
| 1/4 cup granulated sugar | |

Combine gelatin and cold water in a small bowl; let stand 5 minutes to soften. Stir boiling water into gelatin mixture until dissolved. Refrigerate until slightly thickened. In a large bowl, combine condensed milk, granulated sugar and Vanilla Sugar. Using an electric mixer, beat 5 minutes or until thick and foamy. In a medium bowl, beat egg whites until stiff; fold into milk mixture. Fold thickened gelatin mixture into milk mixture. Pour into 4 to 6 dessert dishes. Refrigerate 2 hours or until set. To serve, top with whole strawberries and chocolate curls. Makes 4 to 6 servings.

Illustrations found in this book are based on *wycinanki*, the traditional Polish art of paper cutting. The paper is very thin and has a dull finish on one side and a glossy finish on the other side. The desired design is drawn onto the folded paper, then cut. Once the design is cut, the paper is unfolded, creating a mirrored design.

# Grandmother's Sweet Bread    Photo on pages 2 & 3.

Babka

*This dessert, a cross between cake and sweet bread, is often baked for Easter.*

Topping, see below
3 (1/4-oz.) pkgs. active dry yeast
   (3 tablespoons)
3/4 cup warm water (110F, 45C)
1 tablespoon plus 1 cup sugar
About 7-3/4 cups all-purpose flour
1-1/2 cups milk

1-1/4 cups unsalted butter or margarine
6 eggs
2 egg yolks
1-1/2 teaspoons salt
2 egg whites
Powdered-Sugar Icing, page 141, if desired

*Topping:*
1/4 cup sugar
1/2 cup all-purpose flour
1 teaspoon ground cinnamon

1/4 cup unsalted butter or margarine,
   chilled

Grease side and bottom of 2 (10-inch) tube pans. Prepare Topping; set aside. In a shallow, medium bowl, dissolve yeast in warm water. Add 1 tablespoon sugar and 1/2 cup flour; stir to combine. Cover; let stand in a warm place 5 to 10 minutes until foamy. Heat milk and butter or margarine in a small saucepan until melted. Let stand until mixture cools to warm. In a large bowl, beat eggs, egg yolks and remaining 1 cup sugar until pale and frothy. Add cooled milk mixture, salt and yeast mixture. Beat until smooth. Gradually beat in 4-1/2 cups flour. Stir in enough remaining flour to make a soft dough. Turn out dough on a lightly floured surface. Knead dough into a soft, smooth dough. Divide dough in 1/2. Arrange 1 part dough in each greased pan. Cover with a damp cloth; let rise in a warm place, free from drafts, until doubled in bulk, about 2 hours. Preheat oven to 350F (175C). Lightly beat 2 egg whites in a small bowl until foamy. Brush beaten egg whites on top of dough. Evenly sprinkle Topping over dough. Bake 50 to 55 minutes or until a wooden pick inserted in center comes out clean. Cool cakes in pans 3 to 4 minutes on racks. Turn out of pans; cool completely on racks. Frost with Powdered-Sugar Icing, if desired. Makes 2 (10-inch) cakes.

**Topping:**
In a small bowl, combine sugar, flour and cinnamon. Using a pastry blender or 2 knives, cut in butter or margarine until mixture resembles coarse crumbs.

---

# Vanilla Sugar

Place 2 cups sugar and 2 vanilla beans in a small jar or container. Cover with airtight lid. Set aside in a cool, dry place. Shake occasionally. Store 2 weeks before using. Makes 2 cups.

# Spice Cake

Piernik

*A heavy spice cake, excellent with tea or coffee.*

| | |
|---|---|
| 3-1/2 cups all-purpose flour | 1/2 teaspoon salt |
| 1 tablespoon baking powder | 2 cups plus 3 tablespoons granulated sugar |
| 1/4 teaspoon ground cloves | 1 cup plus 2 tablespoons warm water |
| 1/2 teaspoon ground cinnamon | 2 eggs, separated |
| 1/2 teaspoon ground allspice | Powdered sugar |

Preheat oven to 325F (165C). Grease a 9-inch-square baking pan. Sift together flour, baking powder, cloves, cinnamon, allspice and salt; set aside. In a medium saucepan, combine 2 cups granulated sugar and 1 cup water. Bring to a boil over medium heat, stirring occasionally. Reduce heat to medium-low; cook 10 minutes, stirring constantly. Remove from heat. In a small skillet, place 1 tablespoon sugar. Brown over medium-high heat, about 2 minutes, shaking pan occasionally. Watch carefully to avoid burning sugar. Add 2 tablespoons water; remove from heat. Swirl water until combined with sugar. Add resulting mixture to sugar-syrup in saucepan; stir to blend. Pour sugar mixture into a large bowl. In a small bowl, beat 2 egg yolks and 2 tablespoons sugar vigorously with a fork, about 3 minutes. Stir into sugar mixture. Using an electric mixer, beat sugar mixture 4 to 5 minutes or until smooth. While beating, gradually add flour mixture. In a medium bowl, beat egg whites until stiff peaks form; fold into batter. Pour batter into greased pan. Bake 40 to 45 minutes or until a wooden pick inserted in center comes out clean. Cool cake in pan 2 to 3 minutes on a rack. Turn out of pan; cool completely on rack. Sprinkle with sifted powdered sugar. Do not cut cake until cool. Makes 1 (9-inch-square) cake.

### Variation

When cake cools, slice into 2 layers. Spread 3/4 cup thick plum or cherry jam on top of lower layer. Replace top cake layer. Sprinkle with powdered sugar. Or, frost, if desired.

# Sand Cake

Babka Piaskowa

*This delicious dessert is called sand cake because of its outer texture.*

| | |
|---|---|
| 3/4 cup plus 1 tablespoon butter or margarine | 1/2 teaspoon salt |
| 6 eggs | 1 tablespoon Vanilla Sugar, opposite; or rum extract; or |
| 1 cup granulated sugar | 1 teaspoon vanilla extract |
| 1-2/3 cups all-purpose flour | Sifted powdered sugar |
| 1 tablespoon baking powder | |

Preheat oven to 350F (175C). Grease a 10-inch fluted pan or Bundt pan. Melt butter or margarine in a small saucepan; cool. Using an electric mixer, beat eggs and sugar until pale and creamy, at least 10 minutes on high. Blend in melted butter or margarine. In a small bowl, combine flour, baking powder, salt and Vanilla Sugar, if using. Fold dry ingredients into egg mixture until smooth. If using rum or vanilla extract, stir directly into egg mixture. Pour batter into greased pan. Bake 40 to 45 minutes or until a wooden pick inserted in center comes out clean. Cool cake in pan 2 to 3 minutes on a rack. Turn out of pan; cool completely on rack. Sprinkle with sifted powdered sugar. Makes 1 (10-inch) cake.

# How to Make Sculpture Cake

1/Using your hands, gently press 1/3 of dough evenly over bottom and side of pan. Evenly spread Cheese Filling over lined pan. Roll out another 1/3 of dough to a 10-inch circle. Place dough round over Cheese Filling.

2/Cut remaining 1/3 dough in 4 even pieces. Shape 3 pieces into long ropes. Braid ropes; apply to outer edge of cake. Using remaining dough, cut desired figures with various cutters or form shapes with your hands. Arrange figures on top of dough as desired.

---

# Fancy Fruitcake    Photo on pages 126 & 127.

Keks

*Give these delicious loaves to close friends and relatives for Christmas.*

**1/4 cup dry bread crumbs**
**1-1/2 cups unsalted butter or margarine, room temperature**
**1 cup sugar**
**5 eggs**
**2 tablespoons Polish vodka or other vodka**
**1 tablespoon vanilla extract**

**1-7/8 cups instant flour**
**2 tablespoons baking powder**
**3/4 cup candied orange peel**
**1/2 cup chopped walnuts**
**3/4 cup seedless raisins**
**1/2 cup chopped pitted prunes**

Preheat oven to 350F (175C). Line 2 (8" x 4") bread pans with foil so ends overlap pan sides; grease foil. Sprinkle bread crumbs evenly over greased foil. In a large bowl, beat butter or margarine and sugar 5 minutes or until smooth and creamy. Add eggs, 1 at a time, beating after each addition until smooth. Blend in vodka and vanilla. Reserve 3 tablespoons flour. Gradually add remaining flour and baking powder to mixture, stirring until smooth. In a small bowl, combine orange peel, walnuts, raisins, prunes and reserved flour; toss to coat nuts and fruit. Work fruit and nut mixture into dough. Divide dough between prepared pans. Bake 35 to 40 minutes or until a wooden pick inserted in center comes out clean. Remove loaves from pans by lifting foil. Cool completely on a rack. Makes 2 fruitcakes.

# Sculpture Cake

Kolacz Weselny

*This very old recipe is famous for the artistic, decorative sculpture arranged on top.*

**Cheese Filling, see below**
**2 (1/4-oz.) pkgs. active dry yeast**
  **(2 tablespoons)**
**1 cup plus 1 tablespoon sugar**
**1/4 cup warm water**
**1 cup unsalted butter or margarine,**
  **room temperature**

**2 eggs**
**1 pint warm milk (2 cups)**
**6-1/2 cups all-purpose flour**
**Pinch of salt**
**Milk**

*Cheese Filling:*

**2 lbs. dry cottage cheese or**
  **farmer's old-fashioned white cheese**
  **(4 cups)**

**4 egg yolks**
**2 cups granulated sugar**
**1 tablespoon Vanilla Sugar, page 136**

Prepare Cheese Filling; set aside. In a small bowl, dissolve yeast and 1 tablespoon sugar in 1/4 cup warm water. Let stand 5 to 10 minutes until foamy. Place 1 cup sugar, butter or margarine and eggs in a large bowl. Beat until pale and fluffy. Add yeast mixture, 1 pint milk, 2 cups flour and salt. Beat until well blended. Stir in enough remaining flour to make a soft dough. Turn out dough on a lightly floured surface. Clean and grease bowl. Knead dough until smooth and elastic. Place dough in greased bowl, turning to coat all sides. Cover with a clean damp cloth; let rise in a warm place, free from drafts, until doubled in bulk. Preheat oven to 350F (175C). Grease side and bottom of a 10-inch springform pan. Divide dough into thirds. Using your hands, gently press 1/3 of dough evenly over bottom and side of pan. Evenly spread Cheese Filling over dough-lined pan. On a lightly floured surface, roll out another 1/3 of dough to a 10-inch circle. Place over Cheese Filling. Gently pat with your hands. Using a pastry brush, lightly brush milk over top of dough. Cut remaining 1/3 of dough in 4 even pieces. Shape 3 pieces into long ropes. Braid ropes; apply to outer edge of cake. Using remaining dough, cut desired figures with various cutters or form shapes with your hands. Arrange figures on top of dough as desired. Lightly brush with milk. Bake 50 to 60 minutes or until golden brown. Cool cake in pan 5 minutes on a rack. Remove pan side; cool complete on rack. Makes 1 (10-inch) cake.

**Cheese Filling:**
With a grinder or food processor fitted with a metal blade, process cheese. Do not puree or over process. Place egg yolks, sugar and Vanilla Sugar in a large bowl. Beat until pale and creamy, at least 10 minutes. Add ground cheese, a little at a time, while beating. Beat until smooth.

# Layered Torte

Biszkopt

*Display your artistic skills with this fancy, eye-pleasing torte.*

| | |
|---|---|
| **7 eggs** | **1 tablespoon baking powder** |
| **1-1/8 cups powdered sugar** | **Torte Liquor, see below** |
| **1 tablespoon vinegar** | **Torte Frosting, see below** |
| **2 cups cake flour or all-purpose flour** | |

*Torte Liquor:*

| | |
|---|---|
| **2 cups boiled water, cooled** | **1 tablespoon lemon juice** |
| **2 tablespoons Polish spiritus or rum** | |

*Torte Frosting:*

| | |
|---|---|
| **3 eggs** | **2 tablespoons Polish spiritus or rum** |
| **3/4 cup sugar** | **2 tablespoons lemon juice** |
| **1-1/2 cups unsalted butter or margarine,** | **3 teaspoons instant coffee powder** |
| **room temperature** | **3 tablespoons boiling water** |

Grease a 10-inch springform pan. In a large bowl, beat eggs and sugar 10 minutes or until smooth and fluffy. Add vinegar; beat 2 minutes. Combine flour and baking powder in a medium bowl. Add flour mixture, 1 tablespoon at a time, to beaten egg mixture. Beat well after each addition. Pour batter into pan. Place in a cold oven. Set oven temperature to 350F (175C). Bake 40 to 50 minutes or until a wooden pick inserted in center of cake comes out clean. Do not bump or shake cake during baking because it may fall. Cool in pan 3 to 4 minutes. Remove from pan; cool completely on a rack. Using a long serrated knife, cut cake horizontally into 4 equal layers. Prepare Torte Liquor and Torte Frosting. Sprinkle a little Torte Liquor over each layer. Frost alternate layers of torte with plain and coffee-flavored frosting. Gently stack frosted layers. Spread remaining frosting on side of cake. Use a spatula to swirl frosting. Cover and refrigerate overnight or until frosting sets. Makes 1 (10-inch) cake.

**Torte Liquor:**
Combine water, spiritus or rum and lemon juice in a small bowl.

**Torte Frosting:**
In a medium double boiler over boiling water, combine eggs and sugar. Beat over low heat 10 minutes or until pale and creamy. Remove from double boiler; beat mixture until cool. In a large bowl, beat butter or margarine until creamy. Gradually add egg mixture, beating constantly. Add spiritus or rum and lemon juice; beat until smooth. Divide frosting in 1/2; place in 2 bowls. In a small bowl, dissolve instant coffee in 3 tablespoons water; let cool. Stir dissolved coffee into 1/2 the frosting. Makes enough to frost 1 (10-inch) layered torte.

**Variation**
Substitute 1 tablespoon vanilla extract for 2 tablespoons lemon juice in Torte Frosting.

# Chocolate Cake

Babka Czekoladowa

*The Polish version of one of the most popular cakes in the world.*

5 eggs
1 cup sugar
1 cup plus 2 tablespoons butter or
  margarine, melted
5 oz. semisweet chocolate, melted
Juice of 1/2 lemon

Freshly grated peel of 1 lemon
1-1/2 cups cake flour
1 teaspoon baking powder
1/2 teaspoon baking soda
1/2 teaspoon salt
Chocolate Frosting, see below

*Chocolate Frosting:*
2 teaspoons butter or margarine
3 oz. semisweet chocolate
1 tablespoon water

1 teaspoon lemon juice
1 teaspoon vanilla extract
About 1 cup sifted powdered sugar

Preheat oven to 350F (175C). Grease and flour a 9-inch tube pan. In a large bowl, beat eggs and sugar until pale and creamy. Add butter or margarine, chocolate, lemon juice and lemon peel. Beat at least 5 minutes or until smooth. In a small bowl, sift together cake flour, baking powder, baking soda and salt. Gradually add dry ingredients to egg mixture, beating constantly. Beat until smooth. Pour batter into prepared pan. Bake 45 minutes or until a wooden pick inserted in center comes out clean. Cool cake in pan 2 to 3 minutes on a rack. Turn out of pan; cool completely on rack. Prepare Chocolate Frosting. Drizzle or spread warm frosting over cooled cake. Let stand at room temperature until frosting sets. Makes 1 (9-inch) cake.

**Chocolate Frosting:**
Melt butter or margarine and chocolate in a small saucepan over low heat. Remove from heat. Stir in water, lemon juice and vanilla. Stir about 1 cup powdered sugar into chocolate mixture. If frosting is too thin, add more sifted powdered sugar. If too thick, add a little hot water.

# Powdered-Sugar Icing

Lukier

*The thin, satin-smooth crust of this icing is a nice complement to cookies, mazurkas and cakes.*

2 egg whites
1-1/2 cups sifted powdered sugar

1/2 teaspoon lemon juice

In a medium bowl, beat egg whites until frothy. Gradually add powdered sugar, beating constantly. Beat 10 minutes or until glossy. Add lemon juice; beat 2 minutes or until icing stands up in soft peaks. Makes about 1-1/4 cups icing.

**Variation**

Add food coloring or flavorings, such as 1 teaspoon sifted unsweetened cocoa powder or vanilla extract. Use a little more sugar if liquids are added.

# How to Make Pyramid Cake

1/Add batter to pan, 1/3 cup at a time, baking between each addition, until all batter has been used. Bake until a pick inserted in center comes out clean.

2/Remove cake from pan; let cool on a rack. Makes a delicious cake showing the many layers from baking.

# Pyramid Cake

Sekacz

*Both the consistency and flavor of this attractive cake improve with age.*

3 tablespoons dry bread crumbs
1 cup plus 1 tablespoon unsalted butter or
   margarine, room temperature
1-1/8 cups sugar
7 eggs, separated

1 tablespoon vanilla extract
2 tablespoons rum
1-1/8 cups instant flour
2 teaspoons baking powder
3/4 cup potato starch or cornstarch

Grease a 10-inch tube pan. Evenly sprinkle bread crumbs over bottom. In a large bowl, beat butter or margarine and sugar until light and fluffy, about 5 minutes. Add egg yolks, 1 at a time, beating until smooth after each addition. Beat until pale and fluffy. Add vanilla and rum. Preheat a broiler. Adjust oven rack so top rim of pan is 6 inches from broiler. In a medium bowl, combine instant flour, baking powder and potato starch or cornstarch; fold into egg mixture. Divide resulting mixture into 2 equal parts in 2 medium bowls. Divide egg whites into 2 equal portions; place in 2 other medium bowls. Beat 1 part egg white until stiff but not dry. Fold into 1 part flour mixture, until smooth. Pour 1/3 cup egg-white and flour batter on bottom of prepared pan. Broil 1 to 2 minutes or until golden brown. Remove from oven. Pour another 1/3 cup batter on top of first layer. Return to oven; broil 1 to 2 minutes. Add layers until first portion of batter is used. Prepare second portion of batter by beating remaining egg whites until stiff peaks form; fold into flour mixture. Keep adding and baking thin layers of batter, 1/3 cup at a time, until all batter is used. Insert a wooden pick in center of cake. If pick does not come out clean, broil until pick is clean. Turn cake out of pan; cool on a rack. Makes 1 (10-inch) cake.

# Baked Cheesecake

Sernik

*Chopped walnuts lend a delicious flavor and crispy texture to the crust of this favorite dessert.*

**Crust, see below**
**3 (8-oz.) pkgs. cream cheese,**
  **room temperature**
**1-1/2 cups sugar**
**6 eggs, separated**

**1/4 cup lemon juice**
**1 tablespoon rum extract**
**6 tablespoons all-purpose flour**
**1/2 pint whipping cream (1 cup)**

*Crust:*
**1/4 cup granulated sugar**
**1/4 cup packed brown sugar**
**1/4 cup unsalted butter or margarine,**
  **room temperature**

**3/4 cup all-purpose flour**
**1/4 teaspoon baking powder**
**1/8 teaspoon salt**
**1/2 cup finely chopped walnuts**

Prepare Crust. Preheat oven to 325F (165C). In a large bowl, beat cream cheese 10 minutes or until soft and creamy. Add sugar; beat 3 minutes. Add egg yolks, 1 at a time, beating constantly. Add lemon juice, rum extract and flour; beat until smooth. In a large bowl, beat egg whites until stiff peaks form. Fold beaten egg whites into cheese mixture. Beat whipping cream in a medium bowl; fold into cheese mixture. Pour cheese mixture over baked crust. Bake 1 hour or until a wooden pick inserted in center comes out clean. Turn off oven; let cheesecake stand in oven 1 hour. Remove from oven; cool, then cover and refrigerate 12 hours before serving. Makes 1 (13'' x 9'') cheesecake.

**Crust:**
Preheat oven to 350F (175C). Grease a 13'' x 9'' baking pan. In a large bowl, cream together granulated sugar, brown sugar and butter or margarine. Blend in flour, baking powder, salt and walnuts to form a stiff dough. Press dough evenly over bottom of greased pan. Bake 12 minutes or until golden. Let cool.

# Strawberry Gelatin

Pianka Truskawkowa

*Here's a strawberry recipe that can be prepared year round.*

**1/2 lb. frozen whole strawberries**
**1 tablespoon powdered sugar**
**1 tablespoon unflavored gelatin powder**
**3 tablespoons cold water**

**3 egg whites**
**3 tablespoons granulated sugar**
**Sliced strawberries or thin lemon slices,**
  **if desired**

Place frozen strawberries in a medium bowl; sprinkle with powdered sugar. Let stand 30 minutes or until thawed. Drain thawed-strawberry juice into a small saucepan. Blend gelatin and cold water in a small bowl; let stand 5 minutes or until gelatin is softened. Bring strawberry juice to a boil over medium heat. Stir gelatin mixture into boiling strawberry juice. Refrigerate until slightly thick. In a medium bowl, beat egg whites until soft peaks form. Gradually add granulated sugar, beating constantly until stiff peaks form. Carefully fold strawberries into beaten egg-white mixture. Fold gelatin mixture into egg-white mixture. Refrigerate until set. Serve chilled, decorated with several sliced strawberries or lemon slices, if desired. Makes 4 servings.

# How to Make Crispy-Crust Cheesecake

1/Roughly shred 1 portion of frozen dough evenly onto bottom of pan. Bake 4 to 5 minutes or until golden brown. Let cool. Spoon cheese filling onto baked crust; smooth surface.

2/ Shred remaining portion of frozen dough evenly onto cheese filling. Bake 1-1/2 hours or until a wooden pick inserted in center comes out clean.

# Cool Cheesecake

Sernik na Zimno

*A favorite summer dessert because no baking is involved.*

**3 cups water**
**3 (3-oz.) pkgs. strawberry-flavored gelatin**
**1 lb. farmer's old-fashioned cheese or**
   **dry cottage cheese, drained very dry**
   **(2 cups)**
**1 cup unsalted butter or margarine,**
   **room temperature**

**1-1/8 cups sugar**
**4 eggs, separated**
**Graham crackers or Petit Beurre biscuits**
**About 1 quart fresh strawberries, hulled**

Boil 1-1/2 cups water in a small saucepan. Place gelatin in a medium bowl. Pour boiling water over gelatin; stir until gelatin dissolves. Stir in remaining 1-1/2 cups water. Refrigerate 45 minutes or until thickened but not set. With a hand grinder, grind cheese into a large bowl. In a large bowl, beat butter or margarine and sugar until smooth and creamy. Add egg yolks; beat until smooth. Stir egg-yolk mixture into ground cheese. In a large bowl, beat egg whites until stiff peaks form. Gently fold beaten egg whites and about 2/3 of thickened gelatin into cheese mixture. Line bottom of a 10-inch springform pan with graham crackers or Petit Beurre biscuits, breaking in pieces to fit pan curves. Spoon cheese mixture over crackers or biscuits. Smooth surface with a spoon or wide-bladed knife. Arrange strawberries on cheese mixture. Gently pour remaining gelatin over strawberries. Refrigerate 2 hours or until set. Makes 1 (10-inch) cheesecake.

# Crispy-Crust Cheesecake   Photo on pages 2 & 3.

Sernik

*Of all the Polish cheesecakes, this is one of my favorites.*

Cheesecake Dough, see below
8 eggs, separated
2/3 cup sugar
1-3/4 to 2 cups dry cottage cheese
2 tablespoons unsalted butter or margarine,
    room temperature

2 (8-oz.) pkgs. cream cheese,
    room temperature
1 tablespoon vanilla extract
1 (3-1/2-oz.) pkg. vanilla-pudding mix
Juice of 1 lemon

*Cheesecake Dough:*
1-2/3 cups all-purpose flour
1/2 cup plus 1 tablespoon unsalted butter or
    margarine, chilled
1/3 cup sugar

1 teaspoon baking powder
1 tablespoon sifted unsweetened cocoa powder
1 tablespoon dairy sour cream

Prepare Cheesecake Dough. Cool. Reduce oven temperature to 350F (175C). In a large bowl, beat egg yolks and sugar until pale and creamy. With a hand grinder, grind cottage cheese into large bowl. Add ground cheese, butter or margarine, cream cheese, vanilla, pudding mix and lemon juice to beaten egg-yolk mixture. Beat 8 to 10 minutes or until smooth. In a medium bowl, beat egg whites until stiff but not dry; fold into cheese mixture. Spoon cheese filling onto baked crust; smooth surface. Shred remaining portion of frozen dough evenly over cheese filling. Bake 1-1/2 hours or until a wooden pick inserted in center comes out clean. Cool on a rack at least 2 hours before serving. Makes 1 (10-inch) cake.

**Cheesecake Dough:**
Sift flour into a medium bowl. Using a pastry blender or 2 knives, cut butter or margarine into small pieces; add to flour. Work butter or margarine into flour until mixture resembles coarse crumbs. Add sugar, baking powder, cocoa and sour cream; knead into a smooth dough. Divide dough into 2 equal portions. Wrap both portions in plastic wrap or foil. Place in freezer 30 minutes. Preheat oven to 375F (190C). Grease bottom and side of a 10-inch springform pan. Remove 1 portion dough from freezer. Using a hand shredder, roughly shred 1 portion of frozen dough evenly onto bottom of pan. Bake 4 to 5 minutes or until golden brown.

# Fruit Smoothies

Napoj Owocowy

*A nutritious Polish milkshake.*

1 lb. fresh or frozen strawberries,
    blueberries or pitted cherries
4 egg yolks
3 tablespoons powdered sugar

1 pint milk (2 cups)
Ice cubes
1 teaspoon grated orange peel or lemon peel

Place strawberries, blueberries or cherries in a blender or food processor fitted with a metal blade; process until pureed. Place egg yolks and sugar in a large bowl; beat until fluffy. Add milk, beating until smooth. Add pureed fruit; beat until smooth. Place 2 ice cubes in each of 4 to 6 serving glasses. Pour fruit drink into glasses. Garnish with orange peel or lemon peel. Serve immediately. Makes 4 to 6 servings.

# Poppy-Seed Rolls    Photo on pages 126 & 127.

Strucle z Makiem

*A classic Polish dessert.*

Poppy-Seed Filling, see below
2 (1/4-oz.) pkgs. active dry yeast
   (2 tablespoons)
1/4 cup warm water (110F, 45C)
1 tablespoon granulated sugar
4-1/2 to 5-1/2 cups all-purpose flour
3/4 cup butter or margarine, chilled
2 eggs

3 egg yolks
1/2 cup dairy sour cream
1 cup powdered sugar
1 tablespoon vanilla extract
1/2 teaspoon salt
Grated peel from 1 lemon
1 egg, beaten

*Poppy-Seed Filling:*
1 lb. poppy seeds
1 cup granulated sugar
1 tablespoon Vanilla Sugar, page 136
2 tablespoons butter or margarine
1 egg, slightly beaten
1/4 cup honey

1/4 cup candied orange peel
1/4 cup candied lemon peel
1/2 cup chopped walnuts
1/2 cup golden raisins
2 egg whites

Prepare Poppy-Seed Filling. Grease 2 baking sheets. In a small bowl, dissolve yeast in warm water. Stir in 1 tablespoon granulated sugar and 2 tablespoons flour. Let stand until foamy, 5 to 10 minutes. Sift 4 cups flour into a large bowl. Cut chilled butter or margarine into small pieces; add to flour. Using a pastry blender or 2 knives, cut in butter or margarine until mixture resembles coarse crumbs. Add eggs, egg yolks, sour cream, powdered sugar, vanilla, salt, lemon peel and yeast mixture. Work with your hands or an electric mixer into a soft dough. Turn out dough on a lightly floured surface. Knead dough 8 to 10 minutes or until smooth and elastic. Divide dough into 2 equal parts. On a lightly floured surface, roll each part into a 15- to 16-inch square. Spread Poppy-Seed Filling evenly 2 inches in from all sides of rolled dough. Roll up dough squares jelly-roll style. Pinch ends to seal. Place, seam-side down, on greased baking sheets. Cover and let rise in a warm place, free from drafts, until doubled in bulk. Preheat oven to 350F (175C). Bake 35 minutes. Remove from oven and brush rolls with beaten egg. Bake 5 to 10 minutes longer or until golden brown. Cool rolls on a rack. To serve, slice in 1- or 1-1/2-inch pieces. Makes 2 rolls approximately 17 to 19 inches long.

## Poppy-Seed Filling:

Place poppy seeds in a medium saucepan. Cover with 2 to 3 cups water. Bring to a boil over medium heat. Remove from heat and let stand until cool. Rinse poppy seeds until water is clear, not milky. Carefully strain poppy seeds through a fine-mesh strainer; discard liquid. Stir granulated sugar and Vanilla Sugar into poppy seeds. Using a hand grinder, grind poppy seeds into a medium bowl. Grind seeds 2 more times. Melt butter or margarine in a large skillet. Add poppy-seed mixture. Simmer over low heat 15 to 20 minutes, stirring occasionally. Stir in egg, honey, orange peel, lemon peel, walnuts and raisins. In a medium bowl, beat egg whites until stiff peaks form; fold into poppy-seed mixture. Cool mixture.

## Variations

Substitute 2 (12-1/2-oz.) cans poppy-seed filling for poppy seeds, sugar and Vanilla Sugar. Combine with remaining filling ingredients as directed.

Honey may be omitted for a less sweet filling.

# Nut Roll

Rolada Orzechowa

*One batch makes several rolls; great for entertaining large groups.*

4 (1/4-oz.) pkgs. active dry yeast
   (4 tablespoons)
1/2 cup warm water (110F, 45C)
1/2 cup granulated sugar
1 (12-oz.) can evaporated milk, warmed
7-3/4 cups all-purpose flour
3 eggs
2 cups butter or margarine, melted, cooled

1 teaspoon salt
1 teaspoon vanilla extract
4 lbs. walnuts, finely chopped
1-1/2 cups powdered sugar
1/2 cup honey
1 egg blended with 1 tablespoon
   granulated sugar for glaze

In a medium bowl, dissolve yeast in warm water. Stir in 1/4 cup granulated sugar, milk and 1/4 cup flour. Let stand until foamy, 5 to 10 minutes. In a medium bowl, beat 3 eggs and 1/4 cup granulated sugar until pale and creamy. Stir in melted butter or margarine, salt and vanilla. Stir egg mixture into yeast mixture along with 1 cup flour. Stir in enough remaining flour to make a soft dough. Turn out dough on a lightly floured surface. Clean and grease bowl. Knead dough 8 to 10 minutes or until smooth and elastic, adding flour as needed. Place dough in greased bowl. Cover and refrigerate 3 hours or overnight. In a medium bowl, combine walnuts, powdered sugar and 3/4 cup flour. Divide refrigerated dough into 8 equal portions. Cover and refrigerate 7 parts until needed. Preheat oven to 350F (175C). Grease 2 to 3 large baking sheets. On a lightly floured surface, roll out 1 part dough into an oval about 14'' x 8''. Evenly spread a generous 1 cup walnut mixture over rolled dough. Drizzle 1 tablespoon honey over spread walnut mixture. Working quickly so dough does not get warm, roll up dough lengthwise, jelly-roll style. Place nut roll, seam-side down, on greased baking sheet. Repeat with remaining dough, walnut mixture and honey, arranging nut rolls on greased baking sheets. Allow room for spreading during baking. Bake 15 to 20 minutes or until golden brown. Brush tops of nut rolls with egg glaze immediately upon removal from oven. Cool on a rack. To serve, slice into 1-inch pieces; arrange on a platter. Makes 8 (14- to 16-inch) nut rolls.

# Meringue Crisps

Bezy

*Store these airy sweets in airtight containers to keep them crisp.*

2 egg whites
2/3 cup sifted powdered sugar
1 teaspoon vanilla extract
1 teaspoon lemon juice

1 tablespoon sifted unsweetened cocoa
   powder, if desired
1/4 cup finely chopped walnuts, if desired

Preheat oven to 200F (95C). Grease a baking sheet. Place egg whites in top of a double boiler; beat until stiff. Gradually add powdered sugar, beating constantly. Place double boiler over 1 inch of boiling water. Beat over low heat 8 to 10 minutes or until smooth and glossy. Add vanilla and lemon juice. Add cocoa and walnuts, if desired. Beat 1 minute to blend. Place heaping teaspoon of mixture on greased baking sheet. Or, using a pastry bag fitted with a fluted nozzle, pipe by heaping teaspoon onto baking sheet. Bake about 1-1/4 hours or until hard and crisp; turn oven off and let cool in oven. Makes about 50 cookies.

# Filled Doughnuts

Paczki

*Use your imagination and try any cream or fruit filling that meets your fancy.*

4 (1/4-oz.) pkgs. active dry yeast
  (4 tablespoons)
1/3 cup warm water (110F, 45C)
2 tablespoons plus 1 cup granulated sugar
6-3/4 cups all-purpose flour
1-1/4 cups milk, warmed
12 egg yolks
1 teaspoon salt

1/2 teaspoon vanilla extract
1/2 cup butter, melted, cooled
1/2 cup margarine, melted, cooled
2 tablespoons Polish spiritus or rum
About 3/4 cup thick cherry jam or
  other favorite jam
Vegetable oil
Powdered sugar

Grease 3 baking sheets. In a medium bowl, dissolve yeast in water. Stir in 2 tablespoons granulated sugar and 1/4 cup flour. Blend in milk until smooth. Let stand until foamy, 5 to 10 minutes. In a large bowl, beat egg yolks, 1 cup granulated sugar, salt and vanilla until pale and creamy. Add yeast mixture, melted butter and margarine, 3 cups flour and spiritus or rum. Work mixture into a soft dough, adding flour as needed. Turn out dough on a lightly floured surface. Clean and grease bowl. Knead dough 8 to 10 minutes or until smooth and elastic, working in additional flour as needed. Place dough in greased bowl, turning to coat all sides. Cover and let rise in a warm place, free from drafts, until doubled in bulk, about 2 to 2-1/2 hours. On a flat surface, roll out about 1 cup raised dough until 1/4 inch thick. Keep remaining dough covered to prevent drying. Using a 2-1/2-inch round cutter, cut out dough. Place 1/2 teaspoon cherry jam on 1 dough round. Lightly place another dough round directly on top of the first, covering jam. Using your fingers, crimp dough edges together tightly to prevent halves from separating during frying. Place filled doughnut on a flat working surface. Using a 2-1/4-inch round cutter, press over doughnut so crimped rough edge gets trimmed smooth and round. Place filled doughnut on a lightly greased baking sheet. Repeat process with remaining dough and jam until all baking sheets are filled, being careful to leave enough room between each doughnut for spreading when dough rises. Cover each baking sheet of doughnuts with a clean cloth. Let rise in a warm place, free from drafts, until doubled in bulk, about 1 hour. Pour oil in a deep fryer or large saucepan to a depth of about 5 inches. Heat to 360F (180C) or until a 1-inch bread cube turns golden brown in 60 seconds. Add doughnuts without crowding, raised- or top-side down, so bottom will round out during cooking. Fry 3 to 4 minutes until golden brown. Turn and fry other side about 3 minutes or until golden brown on both sides. Drain on paper towels. Dust doughnuts with powdered sugar. Makes 50 to 60 doughnuts.

# Hot Apple Drink

Kompot z Jablek

*Enjoy this steaming hot beverage after a chilly fall hay ride or winter skiing party.*

2 lbs. firm tart apples, peeled
6 cups water

About 6 tablespoons sugar
6 to 8 (3-inch) cinnamon sticks

Cut each apple into 8 pieces. Place apple pieces and water in a large saucepan; bring to a boil. Reduce heat and simmer, covered, over medium-low heat 15 minutes. Add sugar to taste. Ladle hot liquid and apple pieces into serving cups or glasses. Add a cinnamon stick to each cup or glass. Makes 6 to 8 servings.

# How to Make Filled Doughnuts

1/Place 1/2 teaspoon cherry jam on 1 dough round. Lightly place another dough round directly on top of the first, so jam is covered. Using your fingers, pinch dough edge together very tightly.

2/Place filled doughnut on a flat working surface. Using a 2-1/4-inch round cutter, press over doughnut so crimped rough edge gets trimmed smooth and round.

# Strawberry Soufflé

Suflet Truskawkowy

*An easy-to-prepare, nourishing, delightful dessert.*

**3 eggs, separated**
**3 tablespoons granulated sugar**

**3 tablespoons powdered sugar**
**1 pint fresh strawberries**

Butter 4 ovenproof serving dishes 4'' round by 2-1/2'' deep. Slice large strawberries, if any. Place equal amounts of strawberries in each dish. Preheat oven to 400F (205C). In top of a double boiler, place egg yolks and granulated sugar. Beat over hot water until pale and creamy. Continue beating until warm and starting to thicken. In a large bowl, beat egg whites and powdered sugar until stiff, smooth and glossy. Spoon equal amounts of egg-yolk mixture over strawberries. Carefully spoon egg-white mixture over egg-yolk layers, in equal amounts. Bake 8 to 10 minutes or until golden brown. Serve warm. Makes 4 servings.

# Orange-Lemon Mazurka

Pomaranczowo-Cytrynowy Mazurek

*Aging the crust results in a texture that melts in your mouth.*

2 cups all-purpose flour
1 cup unsalted butter or margarine, chilled
2 egg yolks
3/4 cup powdered sugar
Freshly grated peel of 2 medium oranges

Freshly grated peel of 1 lemon
2 large tart apples, peeled, shredded
1-1/4 cup granulated sugar
1/2 cup slivered almonds

Sift flour into a medium bowl. Cut butter or margarine into small pieces; work into flour until mixture resembles coarse crumbs. Add egg yolks and powdered sugar; work quickly into a rough dough. Press dough into a ball. Wrap and refrigerate 2 hours. Preheat oven to 450F (230C). Grease a 9-inch-square baking pan. On a lightly floured surface, roll dough to a 10-inch square. Using a sharp knife, trim off 1-inch dough from each side; reserve dough scraps. Lightly flour rolled dough; roll onto a rolling pin. Unroll dough into greased pan. Roll remaining dough scraps into a 1/4-inch rope. Arrange dough rope around pan edges on bottom layer of dough, lightly pressing rope into dough. Gently crimp top of dough rope along pan sides, like pie crust. Bake 15 to 20 minutes or until golden brown; cool. Cover and refrigerate 5 or 6 days. Combine orange and lemon peel, shredded apples and granulated sugar in a medium saucepan. Simmer, uncovered, over low heat 20 to 25 minutes or until thick, stirring occasionally. Spoon hot filling over crust. Decorate with slivered almonds; cool. To serve, cut into squares. Makes about 16 servings.

# Honey-Walnut Mazurka     Photo on pages 126 & 127.

Miodowo-Orzechowy Mazurek

*I prepare this rich dessert for friends during the Christmas holidays.*

2-1/2 cups all-purpose flour
2-1/2 cups instant flour
2 teaspoons baking powder
1 cup unsalted butter or margarine, chilled
1 cup granulated sugar
4 egg yolks

1/2 pint dairy sour cream (1 cup)
1 tablespoon vanilla extract
3 cups finely chopped walnuts
1/3 cup powdered sugar
2 cups apricot preserves
1/4 cup honey

In a large bowl, combine all-purpose flour, instant flour and baking powder. Cut butter or margarine into small pieces; add to flour mixture. Work butter or margarine into flour until mixture resembles coarse crumbs. Add granulated sugar, egg yolks, sour cream and vanilla; knead into a smooth dough. Cover with foil or plastic wrap; refrigerate overnight. In a medium bowl, combine walnuts and powdered sugar. Preheat oven to 350F (175C). Divide dough into 3 equal parts. On a lightly floured surface, roll 1 part to a 13'' x 9'' rectangle. Line bottom and sides of a 13'' x 9'' baking pan with waxed paper. Place rolled dough on waxed paper in baking pan. Spread 2/3 cup apricot preserves over dough. Sprinkle 1 cup walnut mixture over apricot preserves. Drizzle 4 teaspoons honey over walnuts. Roll second part of dough to a 13'' x 9'' rectangle. Place on top of first filling layer; press gently to smooth. Repeat filling over second dough layer. Repeat with third layer of rolled dough and filling. Bake 40 to 45 minutes or until top layer of filling becomes a glossy golden brown. Let cool. To serve, cut into squares. Makes 20 to 24 servings.

# Frosted Mazurka

Kaimak Mazurek

*The rich, creamy frosting adds just the right touch to this crispy, cookie-like dessert.*

1-1/2 cups all-purpose flour
1 cup unsalted butter or margarine, chilled
2 egg yolks
1/4 cup powdered sugar
1 tablespoon dairy sour cream

Frosting, see below
Cherries, walnut or pecan halves,
   grated coconut, raisins, candied
   orange peel, dried fruits or
   colored sugar, if desired

*Frosting:*
1-1/2 cups milk
1 cup granulated sugar
1 tablespoon Vanilla Sugar, page 136

1/2 cup unsalted butter or margarine,
   room temperature

Sift flour into a medium bowl. Using a pastry blender or 2 knives, cut butter or margarine into flour until mixture resembles coarse crumbs. Add egg yolks, powdered sugar and sour cream. Work quickly into a rough dough. Press dough into a ball. Wrap and refrigerate 2 hours or overnight. Preheat oven to 350F (175C). Grease a baking sheet. On a lightly floured surface, roll dough to a 13" x 9" rectangle. Lightly flour dough; roll up widthwise on rolling pin. Unroll onto greased baking sheet. Crimp edges like a pie crust. Bake 20 to 25 minutes or until golden. Cool several minutes. If necessary, loosen crust from baking sheet with a spatula. Slide crust onto a clean cutting board; cool. Prepare Frosting. Apply frosting with a long, warm knife for a smooth effect. Or, apply frosting with a spoon and make a swirl effect with bottom of spoon. Garnish with cherries, nuts, coconut, raisins, candied peel, dried fruits or colored sugar, if desired. To serve, cut into squares. Makes about 24 pieces.

**Frosting:**
Combine milk and sugar in a large saucepan. Cook over medium-low heat, stirring occasionally, 35 to 40 minutes or until mixture begins to thicken. Stir Vanilla Sugar into mixture until dissolved. Remove from heat; cool completely. Place butter or margarine in a large bowl; beat until fluffy. Add milk mixture, 1 tablespoon at a time, beating constantly. Beat 2 to 3 minutes longer until smooth.

# Apple Bars    Photo on page 9.

## Szarlotka Krucha

*The classic companion to tea or coffee in Polish homes.*

| | |
|---|---|
| 4 cups all-purpose flour | 8 medium, tart apples, peeled, sliced |
| 1 teaspoon baking powder | 1/4 cup water |
| 1 cup plus 2 tablespoons powdered sugar | 1 tablespoon ground cinnamon |
| 1-1/2 cups plus 2 tablespoons unsalted butter or margarine | 1 cup granulated sugar |
| | 2 tablespoons potato starch or cornstarch |
| 6 egg yolks | 3 tablespoons lemon juice |
| 2 tablespoons dairy sour cream | 3 tablespoons dry bread crumbs |

Sift flour, baking powder and 1 cup powdered sugar into a large bowl. Cut butter or margarine into small pieces; work into flour mixture until mixture resembles coarse crumbs. Add egg yolks and sour cream; work into a firm dough. Press into a ball. Divide dough in 1/2. Cover and refrigerate 1/2 the dough; freeze the other 1/2. To make filling, place apples in a large saucepan; add water. Cover and cook over medium heat 15 minutes. Add cinnamon and granulated sugar. Combine potato starch or cornstarch and lemon juice. Stir into apple mixture. Cook 2 to 3 minutes, stirring frequently, until apple mixture boils and thickens. Preheat oven to 350F (175C). Grease a 13'' x 9'' baking dish. On a lightly floured board, roll refrigerated dough part into a 13'' x 9'' rectangle. Place rolled dough in greased baking dish. Sprinkle bread crumbs over rolled dough. Pour apple mixture on top of crumbs; smooth out apple mixture. Grate frozen dough over apple mixture in an even layer. Bake 55 to 60 minutes or until golden brown. Cool in pan on a rack. Sift 2 tablespoons powdered sugar on top. To serve, cut into squares. Makes 16 to 20 servings.

# Apple Tart

## Szarlotka

*The more tart the apples, the better flavor you will have.*

| | |
|---|---|
| 2-1/2 cups all-purpose flour | 1/2 to 1 cup sugar |
| 1/2 teaspoon salt | 1 teaspoon ground cinnamon |
| 3/4 cup unsalted butter or margarine | 1 teaspoon vanilla extract |
| 5 egg yolks | 3 tablespoons dry bread crumbs |
| 3/4 cup sugar | Sugar |
| 2 lbs. tart cooking apples, peeled | |

In a large bowl, combine flour and salt. Using a pastry blender or 2 knives, cut butter or margarine into small pieces; add to flour. Work butter or margarine into flour until mixture resembles coarse crumbs. Add egg yolks and 3/4 cup sugar; knead into a smooth dough. Cover loosely with foil or waxed paper. Refrigerate 30 minutes. Preheat oven to 350F (175C). Grease a 13'' x 9'' baking pan. Divide dough into 2 equal parts. On a lightly floured surface, roll 1 part dough to a 13'' x 9'' rectangle. Place rolled dough on bottom of greased pan; pat smooth. Bake 10 to 15 minutes or until crust sets. Reduce oven temperature to 325F (165C). Using a coarse blade, grate apples into a large bowl. Add 1/2- to 1 cup sugar to taste, depending on tartness of apples. Stir in cinnamon and vanilla. Sprinkle bread crumbs evenly over crust in pan. Spoon apple filling over bread crumbs; smooth filling. Roll second part of dough to a 13'' x 9'' rectangle. Cut into thin strips. Crisscross dough strips over apple filling. Sprinkle a little sugar on top of dough strips. Bake 50 minutes or until dough strips are browned. Cool on a rack. To serve, cut into squares. Makes 20 to 24 servings.

# How to Make Sweet Crisps

1/Cut dough into an even number of 2-1/2-, 2-, and 1-1/2-inch circles. Score each dough circle 6 to 8 times by slitting from edge to center about 2/3 the distance.

2/Use 1 of each size circle to prepare each rosebud. Dab egg white on center of large circle. Press medium circle onto first, centering. Dab egg white onto center of medium circle. Press on smallest circle. Drop complete rosebuds into hot oil.

# Jam Crescents   Photo on page 152.

## Rogaliki

*Serve this rich, delicate cookie for any tea or special event.*

| | |
|---|---|
| 8 egg yolks | 1 teaspoon baking powder |
| 1 tablespoon dairy sour cream | 1-1/3 cups sifted powdered sugar |
| 1-1/2 cups unsalted butter or margarine, room temperature | About 1/2 cup apricot preserves |
| | 1/2 cup finely chopped walnuts |
| 4-1/2 cups all-purpose flour | 1 egg, lightly beaten |

In a large bowl, beat together egg yolks, sour cream and butter or margarine. Combine flour, baking powder and powdered sugar. Blend dry ingredients into egg mixture, forming a smooth dough. Press dough into a ball. Cover and refrigerate overnight. Preheat oven to 350F (175C). Divide dough into quarters. On a lightly floured board, roll out 1/4 of dough into a rectangle about 1/4 to 1/8 inch thick. Using a sharp knife or pastry wheel, cut into 3-inch triangles. Spread 1/4 teaspoon preserves over each triangle. Sprinkle 1/2 teaspoon walnuts over preserves. Starting at short side of triangle, roll jelly-roll style. Place on an ungreased baking sheet, curving dough to create a crescent shape. Repeat with remaining dough, preserves and walnuts. Brush crescents lightly with egg. Bake 6 to 8 minutes or until tops become golden. Makes 60 to 70 cookies.

# Sweet Crisps    Photo on page 152.

Chrusciki

*These impressive sweet treats will melt in your mouth.*

| | |
|---|---|
| **1 cup all-purpose flour** | **1 tablespoon vodka, whiskey or vinegar** |
| **3 egg yolks** | **Pinch of salt** |
| **3 tablespoons dairy sour cream** | **Vegetable shortening or oil** |
| **1 teaspoon vanilla extract** | **Powdered sugar** |

Place flour in a medium bowl; make a well in center. Add egg yolks; work with your fingertips until blended. Add sour cream, vanilla, liquor or vinegar, and salt. Blend well. On a lightly floured board, work mixture into a smooth dough. Dough should have tiny air bubbles throughout. Cover and refrigerate for later use. For immediate use, on a lightly floured board, roll out dough to about 1/16 inch thick. Slice into 1-1/2-inch-wide strips. Cut strips diagonally into 5-inch lengths. Cut 1-inch slits lengthwise in center of each strip. Pull 1 end of a strip back through slit so strip resembles a bow tie. Repeat procedure with remaining strips. In a large skillet, heat 1-inch-deep vegetable shortening or oil to 375F (190C) or until a 1-inch bread cube turns golden brown in 50 seconds. Deep-fry strips less than 1 minute or until golden, turning once. Drain on paper towels; let cool. Dust with powdered sugar. Serve at room temperature. Makes 12 to 14 dessert servings.

**Variation**    *Photo on opposite page.*

Instead of strips, cut dough into an even number of 2-1/2-, 2- and 1-1/2-inch circles. Score each dough circle 6 to 8 times by slitting from edge to center about 2/3 the distance. Use 1 of each size to prepare each *rosebud*. In a small bowl, lightly beat 1 egg white. Dab egg white on center of 1 large scored dough circle. Press medium scored circle onto first, centering. Dab egg white onto center of medium circle. Press on smallest circle. Repeat procedure until all *rosebuds* are made. Drop completed *rosebuds* into hot oil as above, smallest circle down. Fry as above. Decorate with a dusting of powdered sugar and by placing a maraschino cherry, dab of jam, or dollop of chocolate in center of top.

# Sponge Cookies    Photo on page 152.

Biszkopty

*These crisp, light cookies are especially delicious when served with ice cream.*

| | |
|---|---|
| **5 eggs, separated** | **1/2 teaspoon salt** |
| **1 cup sugar** | **1-1/2 cups all-purpose flour** |

Preheat oven to 350F (175C). Grease or line with parchment paper 2 baking sheets. In large bowl of an electric mixer, beat egg yolks and sugar until creamy, about 5 minutes on high. Combine salt and flour in a sifter. Continue to beat egg mixture on high, gradually sifting in flour mixture. In a medium bowl, beat egg whites until stiff but not dry. Beat 1/3 of beaten egg whites into batter. Fold in remaining beaten egg whites until smooth with no egg white showing. Spoon mixture into a pastry bag fitted with a large plain nozzle. Pipe 3-1/2-inch long cookies onto greased or parchment-lined baking sheets, leaving space between each cookie for spreading during cooking. Bake 15 to 20 minutes or until light golden. Cool cookies on baking sheets 3 to 4 minutes. Transfer to a rack to cool completely. Makes about 40 cookies.

# Cream Tarts

Babeczki Smietankowe

*A favorite dessert of children, especially when decorated with funny faces.*

**Individual Tart Shells, see below**
**6 eggs**
**1 tablespoon vanilla extract**
**1/4 cup all-purpose flour**

**2/3 cup sugar**
**2 cups milk**
**Raisins, cherries or walnut halves,**
  **if desired**

*Individual Tart Shells:*
**1/2 cup sugar**
**1 cup butter or margarine, room temperature**

**1 egg**
**2 cups all-purpose flour**

Prepare Individual Tart Shells. In top of a double boiler, beat eggs and vanilla together. Combine flour and sugar; add gradually to egg mixture, beating constantly. In a medium saucepan, bring milk to a boil over medium-high heat. Remove from heat as soon as milk begins to boil. Add milk to egg mixture, a little at a time, until all milk is added. Bring 2- to 3-inches water to a boil in bottom of double boiler. Cook egg mixture over boiling water, stirring constantly, until smooth, glossy and the consistency of pudding, about 15 minutes. Let cool. Spoon equal amounts of cooled egg mixture into each cooled baked tart shell. Decorate as desired. Refrigerate tarts before serving. Makes 18 to 20 tarts.

**Individual Tart Shells:**
Preheat oven to 350F (175C). Beat together sugar, butter and egg until light and fluffy. Gradually add flour until blended and smooth. Turn out dough on a lightly floured surface. Divide dough into 3 parts. Pinch off small pieces and press into 2-1/2 inch tartlet pans. Or, roll 1 dough portion until 1/4 to 3/8 inch thick. Using a small plastic lid or inverted bowl as a guide, cut 4-inch circles. Set scraps aside. Roll out remaining portions of dough, cutting as many circles as possible. Gently knead all dough scraps together. Roll out and cut more circles for a total of 18 to 20 circles. Gently press each circle into a 2-3/4-inch muffin cup, making evenly spaced tucks around edge of each circle. Bake 20 minutes or until golden. Cool in pan 2 to 3 minutes on a rack. Remove from pans; cool completely on rack.

# Flavored Fruit Gel

Kisiel

*A refreshingly cool, thick dessert with a delicious fruit flavor.*

**1 qt. fresh raspberries or red currants**
**1 cup cold water**
**2 tablespoons sugar**

**1-1/2 tablespoons potato starch or**
  **cornstarch**
**1/2 cup cold water**

Place raspberries or currants and 1 cup cold water in a medium saucepan. Bring to a boil over medium-high heat. Reduce heat to low. Simmer, uncovered, stirring occasionally 20 minutes. Stir sugar into simmering berry mixture. In a small bowl, blend potato starch or cornstarch and 1/2 cup cold water. Strain cooked berries through a fine-mesh strainer into a medium bowl; extract cooking juices then discard seeds and pulp. Stir starch mixture into strained cooking liquids. Place resulting strained mixture in a medium saucepan. Bring to a boil over medium heat, stirring constantly. Pour into small serving dishes or pudding dishes. Refrigerate 2 or more hours before serving. Makes 4 to 6 servings.

# INDEX

# POLISH RECIPE TITLES

# Metric Chart

## Comparison to Metric Measure

| When You Know | Symbol | Multiply By | To Find | Symbol |
|---|---|---|---|---|
| teaspoons | tsp | 5.0 | milliliters | ml |
| tablespoons | tbsp | 15.0 | milliliters | ml |
| fluid ounces | fl. oz. | 30.0 | milliliters | ml |
| cups | c | 0.24 | liters | l |
| pints | pt. | 0.47 | liters | l |
| quarts | qt. | 0.95 | liters | l |
| ounces | oz. | 28.0 | grams | g |
| pounds | lb. | 0.45 | kilograms | kg |
| Fahrenheit | F | 5/9 (after subtracting 32) | Celsius | C |

## Liquid Measure to Milliliters

| | | |
|---|---|---|
| 1/4 teaspoon | = | 1.25 milliliters |
| 1/2 teaspoon | = | 2.5 milliliters |
| 3/4 teaspoon | = | 3.75 milliliters |
| 1 teaspoon | = | 5.0 milliliters |
| 1-1/4 teaspoons | = | 6.25 milliliters |
| 1-1/2 teaspoons | = | 7.5 milliliters |
| 1-3/4 teaspoons | = | 8.75 milliliters |
| 2 teaspoons | = | 10.0 milliliters |
| 1 tablespoon | = | 15.0 milliliters |
| 2 tablespoons | = | 30.0 milliliters |

## Liquid Measure to Liters

| | | |
|---|---|---|
| 1/4 cup | = | 0.06 liters |
| 1/2 cup | = | 0.12 liters |
| 3/4 cup | = | 0.18 liters |
| 1 cup | = | 0.24 liters |
| 1-1/4 cups | = | 0.3 liters |
| 1-1/2 cups | = | 0.36 liters |
| 2 cups | = | 0.48 liters |
| 2-1/2 cups | = | 0.6 liters |
| 3 cups | = | 0.72 liters |
| 3-1/2 cups | = | 0.84 liters |
| 4 cups | = | 0.96 liters |
| 4-1/2 cups | = | 1.08 liters |
| 5 cups | = | 1.2 liters |
| 5-1/2 cups | = | 1.32 liters |

## Fahrenheit to Celsius

| F | C |
|---|---|
| 200—205 | 95 |
| 220—225 | 105 |
| 245—250 | 120 |
| 275 | 135 |
| 300—305 | 150 |
| 325—330 | 165 |
| 345—350 | 175 |
| 370—375 | 190 |
| 400—405 | 205 |
| 425—430 | 220 |
| 445—450 | 230 |
| 470—475 | 245 |
| 500 | 260 |